What people are saying

Introducing the Oc

Colin Wilson was one of the most generous of writers, and by this I don't mean his prolific output, but the amount of time and effort he devoted to promoting the work of others. That largesse is well in evidence in this collection of Wilson's introductions to some of the many works on the supernatural and esoteric that came in the wake of his classic on the subject, *The Occult*, brought together by his friend and bibliographer, Colin Stanley. Readers of *Mysteries*, *Beyond the Occult*, *Poltergeist!*, *Afterlife*, and Wilson's other works about the frontiers of consciousness, will be delighted to find a batch of significant essays on a number of subjects that might otherwise be unavailable to them. And if they haven't already, they might also be led back to the books themselves. I know it was practically always the case that if Wilson gave a book his imprimatur, it was worth reading. It goes without saying that this collection is too.
**Gary Lachman**, author of *Beyond the Robot: the life and work of Colin Wilson.*

Colin Wilson was the most exciting and readable non-fiction author of the 20th century, whose mind was so wide-ranging that he was equally at home in philosophy, criminology and parapsychology. This is an essential collection of some of his lesser known writings, all of which display his remarkable gifts as a writer and thinker.
**Steve Taylor** PhD, author of *The Leap* and *Spiritual Science.*

*Introducing the Occult* is a treasure trove for those interested in esoteric wisdom. Colin Wilson helped introduce hundreds of authors' books to the world, and in each essay or introduction, he honed his own philosophy and expanded on his extraordinary insights into human consciousness. This book, like the celebrated *The Occult*, offers an accessible and highly readable guide to the sometimes shadowy and obscure world of occultism. Colin Stanley, Wilson's indefatigable bibliographer, has done us all a favour by gathering these wide-ranging and life-changing insights together all in one volume.

**David J. Moore**, author of *Evolutionary Metaphors: UFOs, New Existentialism and the Future Paradigm.*

# Introducing the Occult

Selected Introductions, Prefaces,
Forewords and Afterwords

# Introducing
# the Occult

Selected Introductions, Prefaces,
Forewords and Afterwords

## Colin Wilson

Selected, Edited and Introduced by

## Colin Stanley

AXIS MUNDI
BOOKS

Winchester, UK
Washington, USA

JOHN HUNT PUBLISHING

First published by Axis Mundi Books, 2022
Axis Mundi Books is an imprint of John Hunt Publishing Ltd., 3 East Street, Alresford,
Hampshire SO24 9EE, UK
office@jhpbooks.com
www.johnhuntpublishing.com
www.johnhuntpublishing.com/axismundi-books

For distributor details and how to order please visit the 'Ordering' section on our website.

ISBN: 978 1 78099 475 8
978 1 78099 476 5 (ebook)
Library of Congress Control Number: 2021942547

A CIP catalogue record for this book is available from the British Library.

Design: Stuart Davies

UK: Printed and bound by CPI Group (UK) Ltd, Croydon, CR0 4YY
Printed in North America by CPI GPS partners

We operate a distinctive and ethical publishing philosophy in
all areas of our business, from our global network of authors to
production and worldwide distribution.

# Contents

Related books by Colin Wilson:

*The Occult.* 978-1-78028846-8
*Mysteries.* 978-1-78678-349-3
*Beyond the Occult.* 978-1-78678-348-6
*Super Consciousness.* 978-1-78678-288-5
*The Ultimate Colin Wilson.* 978-1-78678-253-3

Related books by Colin Stanley:

*Around the Outsider: essays presented to Colin Wilson on the occasion of his 80th birthday.* 978-1-84694-668-4
*Colin Wilson's 'Occult Trilogy': a guide for students.*
978-1-84694-706-3
*An Evolutionary Leap: Colin Wilson on Psychology.*
978-1-7822044-4-2
*Proceedings of the First International Colin Wilson Conference.*
978-1-4438-8172-2
*Reflections on the Work of Colin Wilson: Proceedings of the Second International Colin Wilson Conference.*
978-1-5275-2774-4

# Editor's Introduction

Astonishingly Colin Wilson wrote over 180 introductions, forewords, prefaces and afterwords to other authors' books. I struggle to think of any author who has dedicated more time to the promotion of the work of his friends and colleagues. And, as this volume reveals, these were not hurriedly written paragraphs, relying largely on his name as an endorsement, but often significant and substantial essays.

When his extraordinary study *The Occult* appeared in 1971, several readers, enthused by his previous books on existentialist philosophy, accused him of abandoning the rigours of his 'Outsider Cycle' for a much more trivial pursuit. He replied:

> "...such a view was incomprehensible. It seemed obvious to me that if the 'paranormal' was a reality—as I was increasingly convinced that it was—then any philosopher who refused to take it into account was merely closing his eyes."

Of course, Colin Wilson had *not* abandoned philosophy at all. This is clearly portrayed in his fascinating preface to Dr David Foster's book *The Intelligent Universe*, written in 1975, which I have included as an appendix to this volume. Indeed, he always considered his 'serious' occult books to be a logical extension of his 'new existentialism', providing evidence that man possesses latent powers which, if tapped and harnessed, could lead to hugely expanded consciousness and potentially even an evolutionary leap. He went on to write two more large books on the subject: *Mysteries* (1978) and *Beyond the Occult* (1988) which came to be known as his 'Occult Trilogy' and are now acknowledged classics in the field of the Occult Sciences. The three books amounted to a monumental 1600 pages and spawned many other lesser works on the subject.

1

As a result, he was constantly sought out by authors and publishers to endorse their work. He rarely refused. I recall asking him once why he devoted so much of his valuable time (often without any thought of financial reward) to writing these endorsements. He replied that, as a child, he had noticed that one of his favourite authors, G. K. Chesterton, often wrote introductions and had decided then that, if he became a writer, he would do likewise.

Colin Stanley
Nottingham, UK
March 2021

N.B. The letter and number in brackets following each title (e.g. D43) refers to that item in my two-volume *The Post-Ultimate Colin Wilson Bibliography, 1956–2020*. Nottingham: Paupers' Press, 2020.

# 1

# Introduction: *The Search for Abraxas* (D9)

by Nevill Drury and Steven Skinner
Sudbury, Suffolk: Neville Spearman, 1972
New edition: The Golden Hoard Press, 2016.

It is difficult to maintain a sense of historical perspective about your own epoch. Too much is happening; there are too many trends and events and intellectual fashions, and you can never be sure which of them will appear important in a hundred years' time. But it has been borne in upon me recently that a pretty spectacular change really has taken place in the past ten or fifteen years—as total and unexpected as some of the great climatic changes of the Pleistocene. When I was writing my first book, at the age of 23 (in 1955), both Europe and America were in the middle of a phase of 'political consciousness'. Most of the intelligent young people were concerned about the bomb and germ warfare, and a few were even then concerned about overpopulation and pollution of the environment. They marched to Aldermaston, and signed protests about South Africa, and turned up in Trafalgar Square to boo Sir Oswald Mosley when he made speeches about the necessity for Britain to join Europe in a single economic community.

I felt completely out of it, since politics interested me less than poetry, music, and religion. This was not a reasoned attitude; it was purely instinctive. I labelled the problem 'the Bombard effect', after the Frenchman Alain Bombard, who sailed a rubber dinghy across the Atlantic in the early fifties, living entirely on plankton and the juices squeezed from fishes. Half-way across, Bombard made the mistake of going on board a passing ship and eating a good meal; it almost cost him his life, for when he got back into his dinghy, the meals of plankton and squashed fish made him vomit for days before his stomach readjusted.

This, I felt, was the problem that destroyed Shelley and Novalis and Hölderlin and Van Gogh. They had experienced states of mind in which life suddenly became infinitely interesting, in which a tree became a torch of green flame and a night sky a whirlpool of pure vitality. Then they were asked to return to 'ordinary consciousness' and the boundless mediocrity of our commercial civilisation. No wonder they vomited themselves into a state of mental exhaustion. As to me, I half envied these left-wing protesters and marchers; their stomachs were obviously healthier and stronger than mine. For me, their Marxist slogans were only one degree less nauseating than the bomb itself.

For the remainder of the fifties, and well into the sixties, the left-wing novelists, playwrights and critics had it all their own way—Amis, Braine, Doris Lessing, Osborne, Wesker, Logue, Tynan and the rest. (I am confining myself to England, but most other countries could make up their own lists.) They seemed unanswerable: that in a world with so many starving people, so many problems requiring political action, it was the worst kind of irresponsibility to find Dostoevsky and Hesse more interesting than Brecht and Sholokov. They were never slow to point out that such a preference verged on fascism (although I could never follow the logic of this argument).

Oddly enough, the philosophical position of these leftists was often curiously pessimistic. They were inclined to accept Freud's disheartening view of human nature: that culture is man's attempt to compensate for the dark forces of the libido, and that the fundamental striving of life is towards death. When Genet compared society to a brothel for perverts, they cheered; when Ionesco and Beckett said that life was meaningless anyway, they nodded sadly. In a sense, this was logical; for if life is as dreary and meaningless as they seemed to think, then there is nothing more important than achieving a fair distribution of wealth.

All this aggressive left-wingery made life somewhat difficult, both for me and for friends who shared my attitudes, like Bill Hopkins and Stuart Holroyd. Our books got panned by critics, who accused us of obscurantism, neo-fascism, lack of social responsibility. I once pointed out that even Sartre, that inveterate leftist, makes Mathieu, the hero of *Roads to Freedom*, speak about the need for individual 'salvation', whereupon a critic replied that Sartre had intended Mathieu to be an example of a bourgeois weakling....

What precisely happened then? I'm damned if I know. All I know is that I continued to write books, and they ceased to be attacked, and were simply ignored. The tide seemed to be as far out as it possibly could be. Then, round about 1966 or 67, the change began. For example, to the amazement of his English and American publishers, the novels of Hermann Hesse began to sell in huge quantities. He had been dead since 1962, and although he had received the Nobel Prize in 1946, it could be said that he had been half-forgotten since the thirties. His novels about individuals who take to the road in search of 'salvation' were apparently as old-fashioned as Galsworthy and Hergesheimer. When I decided to write about Hesse in *The Outsider* in 1954, all his novels were out of print in English, and I had to read them in the British Museum reading room. After the brief fashionable success of *The Outsider*, Hesse's novels began to be reprinted, and American dons wrote articles about him in academic publications (although their bibliographies never included *The Outsider*); but it was still a mere trickle of interest. Then the trickle became a flood, and Hesse again became a best-seller, as he had been in the twenties in Germany.

What seems to have happened is that the beatnik movement, started in America by Kerouac and Ginsberg as a drop-out revolt against bourgeois respectability and the American

5

Dream, outgrew its original anti-intellectualism—the cult of Charlie Parker, Billie Holiday, James Dean—and began to set up a pantheon of intellectual idols that included figures as disparate as Marcuse and Tolkien. The faces on the Beatles' *Sergeant Pepper* LP include Aleister Crowley, Jung, Poe and Aldous Huxley. Poe one can understand—the outsider who died of neglect in a society interested only in money. And Aldous Huxley, who was the real founder of the psychedelic cult with his 1953 book on mescalin. But Jung, with his obscure German syntax, and Crowley, that Dionysian Kabbalist who was mistakenly labelled a Satanist—how on earth did they manage to seep into the consciousnesses of the pop enthusiasts? I would as soon have expected to find pictures of Einstein or Musil on the LP jacket.

By the late sixties, it was very clear that the Jung-Crowley combination represented a new current of interest. There had always been a small, specialist market for books on occultism. In the early fifties, Rider and Co. of London republished the magical works of Eliphaz Levi, Muldoon on astral projection, and biographies of Hindu mystics; but the market was always sluggish. Ten years later, in America, University Books re-published the books of A. E. Waite, Yeats's associate in the Golden Dawn society, and Montague Summers' treatises on vampires and witchcraft. My old friend August Derleth had kept the works of H. P. Lovecraft in print since his death in 1937, but his customers almost amounted to a Lovecraft Book Club; you couldn't walk into a bookshop and buy them off the shelves. I suspect that the audience for all these books remained about as large as the audience for LP records of train noises. Then, suddenly, it began to grow. Works like Regardie's four-volume *Golden Dawn*, which could have been purchased for five quid in 1950, was so much in demand that it became worth eighty pounds a set. Early in 1970, a publisher of part-magazines (i.e., magazines intended to be collected and eventually bound

6

into volumes) embarked on an apparently rash project, the publication of an alphabetical encyclopaedia of magic and occultism in 112 weekly parts; *Man, Myth and Magic* amazed the publishing trade by becoming the magazine equivalent of a best-seller—so successful that it has now been reprinted in twenty-five volumes.

But even the publishers of these books and magazines found it difficult to explain the precise nature of this enthusiasm. On the surface, it seemed to be the shallow, fashionable, completely unaccountable interest that creates best-sellers. All you can say is that it often seems to be bound with escapism—the Kon Tiki expedition, Jacques Cousteau's undersea adventures, and so on. This certainly seemed to be the case in 1960, when Gallimard brought out in Paris a curious work called *Le Matin des Magiciens* by Louis Pauwels and Jacques Bergier. The book sold and sold, yet its success was difficult to explain. For this was no closely reasoned work on the paranormal, but a kind of resembling Ripley's *Believe it Or Not*. The book swoops from quantum theory to the mythology of Lovecraft, from buried cities in the Brazilian jungle to the suggestion that the Nazis were an occult society. A fascinating book, certainly; but the kind of thing that would enrage any logical positivist because its authors seem to have an attitude of blissful indifference towards questions of proof and verification. The English and American editions, published three years later, had nothing like the same success; but they may have been responsible for starting the occult craze that snowballed during the next seven years.

Readers of Sunday newspapers were inclined to believe that all the talk about witch cults was an invention of journalists. Not that anyone doubted the existence of such cults; everyone knew that the works of the late Gerald Gardner—which purported to describe witch cults already in existence—had led to the formation of dozens of such covens. But the general opinion was that these were either harmless religious organisations, practising pagan nature worship by the light of the moon, or excuses for voyeurism and sexual orgies. (Gardner was himself a voyeur.) The new interest in Crowley seemed to be merely another expression of the anti-authoritarianism of the young. For Crowley, as he emerges in John Symonds' biography *The Great Beast*, seems to be a martyr to the romantic-artistic principle of shocking the bourgeoisie. His life was apparently spent cocking a snook at respectability, and respectability reacted by treating him as the outcast he seemed determined to become.

In fact, this whole notion was mistaken. And this brings me, belatedly, to the subject of the present book, and its two young authors. For what readers of *The Great Beast* could be forgiven for failing to understand was that, exhibitionist or not, Crowley was as dedicated and serious a magician as Einstein was a physicist. He belonged to a tradition that believed wholly in the objective efficacy of magic.

I must emphasise this, for readers of this introduction will miss the whole point if they fail to grasp it. We are not talking about Rhine's experiments in extra-sensory perception, or about naked girls copulating with a high priest on an altar. We are talking about a belief that has been discredited for the past three centuries, but which has never ceased to be accepted by a small number of men and women, that certain magical operations can produce a result in nature—as when the North Berwick witches confessed to causing the storm that almost wrecked the fleet of James VI of Scotland when he was returning from Denmark with his newly married bride. We dismiss this as pure delusion. And no practising magician would deny that it could have been pure delusion. But, he would insist, there are forces in nature, and in the human mind, which can be called upon through certain magical disciplines, which could cause such a storm. In fact, the more I study the case of the North Berwick witches, the more I am inclined to doubt my original opinion that they were persecuted innocents. There are now plenty of highly convincing accounts of Africans who can call up a storm through tribal ceremonies, and it strikes me as a real possibility that the North Berwick witches may have discovered how to work the same trick.

There are, nowadays, hundreds of serious students of magic who believe that the magicians of the past were really 'on to something': that is a half-forgotten tradition, as alien to our modes of thinking as Balinese music is to ears accustomed to western music. Their belief rests on two premises, one more-or- less acceptable to the western mind, the other totally unacceptable. The acceptable premise is that the human mind is bigger and stranger than any psychologist has ever guessed—although Jung came close to it—and that it possesses unexplored powers. They also believe that there is a purely objective component in magic; that there are 'powers and dominions' in nature, god-like or demonic forces, that can be utilised by the human mind when it has learned to draw upon its hidden powers. This notion is, of course, offensive to the western intellect, although most regions accept something of the sort. (As I write this, the Bishop of Exeter has just created something of a sensation by recommending that all parishes should possess an exorcist for casting out spirits and demons.)

A whole school of young practising magicians has sprung up. They are not sensation-seekers or hippies. They pursue their subject with the same seriousness that they might study electronic engineering or radio astronomy. They attempt to control the mind and discipline the imagination, assuming that such discipline may bring into being higher levels of consciousness that in turn may focus and control powers that are inaccessible to ordinary consciousness. You could say that the basic principle is the feeling that 'everyday consciousness' is like a cloud of gnats, all flying aimlessly, changing direction yet maintaining a general shape and position. Magic begins by assuming that these aimless energies could be channelised and ordered, and that the result might be totally unlike anything you could anticipate from studying the behaviour of a cloud of gnats. No one could judge an orchestra from the sounds it makes while tuning up; yet we commit an analogous mistake about the human mind. Or again, we know that ordinary light consists of a mass of tangled energies like a ball of cotton wool; but when these energies have been untangled and brought into step through a ruby laser, the resulting light has the power to cut through metal.

W. B. Yeats has written in his autobiographies of his membership of the magical society called the Order of the Golden Dawn; and ever since Yeats was acknowledged as the greatest of modern Irish poets, commentators have discussed his 'magical' affiliations as if they were a sign of charming eccentricity, the poet's ability to believe a dozen untrue things before breakfast. What had become clear in the past few years is that this view was mistaken; the Golden Dawn was a genuine magical society, bringing to its own experiments the same seriousness that Lord Rutherford brought to the investigation of crystal structures. Moreover, these younger students of magic have taken up where Mathers and Waite left off. Francis King's *Ritual Magic in England* discusses some of these recent groups and records their claim that they have actually produced 'results'.

The young authors of this present book regard themselves as serious students of the magical tradition. Both live in Australia. Stephen Skinner, born in 1948 in Sydney, is a graduate from Sydney University who is at present a lecturer in a technical College. Nevill Drury, born in 1947, was born in Hastings, Sussex, and has spent half his life in Australia; he is a graduate of Sydney University, and majored in anthropology and modern history. They seem to have approached 'occultism' from opposite positions. Nevill Drury thinks of himself as basically an artist (hence his interest in Austin Spare). His father is an art lecturer at Perth, and Nevill's coloured ink drawings have been on exhibition in Sydney. He became interested in magic through *Le Matin des Magiciens* and the works of Arthur Machen; he also edited the Australian *UFO Review* from 1966 to 1969. A grandmother was an ardent Steinerite, and his father came under the influence of Buddhist thought while serving as an officer in the Second World War.

Stephen Skinner began as a student of psychology; in a letter to me, he commented that he found MacDougall's *Abnormal Psychology* and Sinclair's studies in philosophy inadequate to explain the observed phenomena of the mind. The behaviourist psychology he encountered at university also left him thoroughly dissatisfied, since it 'seemed to lose sight of the psyche in a maze of stats and Skinner boxes'. The psychological need for more 'nutritious' objects of study led him to works on occultism, and on the Qabalah in particular. This highly complex and precise system of mysticism satisfied the need for logical exactitude, and he came to concentrate on Qabalism. The Qabalah prescribes various practical disciplines for exploring 'astral' realms; it might be described as a form of occult behaviourism.

It was at this point that Skinner and Drury met — at university — and Drury was impressed by Skinner's Qabalistic erudition (although, as an artist, he finds the theoretical side of Qabalism less interesting than its symbolic and 'intangible' aspects). Drury's belief that the artist is a vehicle for, not a creator of, his artistic productions, produced a desire to explore methods of charting the hidden sources of inspiration.

"The levels of inspiration achieved by different artists seems to me to parallel the stages of consciousness outlined in the Qabalah, and for this reason, one of my main aspirations is to achieve greater rapport with the higher levels of my unconscious."

11

And so Skinner's need for scientific exactitude and Drury's desire to tap hidden levels of subconscious vitality combine in a common purpose. The first result of their cooperation appears in this far-ranging and highly readable book.

To the casual reader, the result will probably seem as vertiginous—if as absorbing—as *Le Matin des Magiciens*. The discussion moves swiftly from Ballou's *OAHSPE*, a book supposedly written at the dictation of an angel, through sketches of gnosticism and Qabalistic philosophy, to a number of studies of the borderland between art and occultism—especially in the art of Austin Spare, who fascinates both writers.

What the authors have attempted to do, in the briefest possible space, is to present the basis of their studies, the core of their obsessions. They might have attempted a more massive structure, discussing the Qabalah in detail, and attempting to relate the work of various artists to its 'levels of consciousness'. But at the present stage, such a labour would probably be premature. Instead, they have chosen the intuitive method of presentation, to discuss what deeply interests them, leaving the reader to divine all the connections. In some cases, these connections are clear enough. For example, the description of the experiences of Carlos Castaneda as the pupil of a Yaqui Indian 'witch doctor' make clear the connection between the Qabalah, the witch cults of the Middle Ages, and the use of hallucinogenic drugs. Sceptics will argue that such experiences— as soaring through the air—could only be produced by drugs, and prove nothing whatever about the reality of 'other' states of consciousness. Drury and Skinner argue that such experiences allow us to glimpse the active powers of the imagination, and that the realms of consciousness glimpsed by Castaneda are an objective reality that can also be explored by Qabalistic disciplines.

The authors of this book represent a new phenomenon: the serious study of the practice of magic. (Another young writer,

David Conway, has presented a more systematic exploration of the methods in *Magic, An Occult Primer*, which again lays central emphasis upon the training and control of imagination.)* It is true that 'occult revivals' seem to have occurred in the last decades of the past three centuries, as a reaction against the current of rationalism. What is so interesting about this latest wave of occultism is it is more sober and rational than any of its predecessors. These practising magicians have decided that there is something in magic, something as objective as radio waves. They have set out to investigate it in a spirit in which Yeats's romanticism combines with scientific empiricism. They seem determined to get to the bottom of it, or at least, to go further in understanding it than any of their predecessors have attempted, using the discoveries of anthropology, as epitomised in the work of Eliade and Levi-Strauss, and the insights of Jungian psychology. And this seems to me logical, even predictable. In *Religion and the Rebel*, I pointed out that science began as the study of distant phenomena, the stars and planets. Then it moved down to earth, with physics and chemistry. Later came geology, then biology, then psychology, then the social sciences. At each stage there has been a time-lag before these subjects were regarded as respectable enough to teach in universities; man found it hard to believe that anything so close to him as psychology or sociology could be a real science. With each new science, the focus moves further from the outside universe, in towards man himself. A century ago, it would have been as impossible to take a scientific attitude towards magic as it was for the Victorians to take a scientific attitude towards sexual perversion. It was a bit too near the bone.

Now, at last, we have some of the necessary tools for analysing 'the facts'. The problem now is to find out precisely what the facts are. What Stephen Skinner and Nevill Drury have done in this book is not to make an anthology of the weird and wonderful, but to state, with a kind of modesty and quiet precision, what they consider the relevant 'facts' to be. It is their manifesto, and the manifesto of a new generation. What will spring from it remains to be seen.

**Notes:**

* For Colin Wilson's introduction to this book: see Chapter 7. *Ed.*

# 2

# Introduction: *The Magicians: Occult Stories* (D11)

edited by Peter Haining
London: Peter Owen, 1972

The last great 'magical revival' took place in France towards the end of the nineteenth century and spread from there to Germany and England. When it petered out, round about 1900, it seemed a fair assumption that the western world had finally seen the last of magic. When I became interested in the subject— in 1950—I would certainly have taken a bet on it. And now, as we enter the seventies, we suddenly find ourselves in the midst of another 'occult revival', as unexpected and as unexplainable as the ones that preceded it.

For this is the odd thing about these revivals—that they seem to be so weirdly unpredictable. The great age of witchcraft came to an end in the late 1600s, and the age of Newton and Leibniz and Priestley began. In 1750, any historian who predicted a magical revival would have been regarded as mad; but by 1770, Cagliostro and St Germain and Mesmer were on the scene, and astrologers and alchemists were as popular as two centuries earlier. With the death of Cagliostro in the papal prison in 1795, the 'revival' stopped as abruptly as it had begun. A new age of science and industry dawned; the 'Dark Satanic Mills' roared day and night. (And Blake's 'Satanic Mills' are not those of the industrial revolution, but of logic and science.) Surely the age of magic was at an end? Then the Fox sisters began their spirit rapping; Daniel Dunglas Home made tables float in the air; Eliphas Levi conjured up the spirit of Apollonius of Tyana; the sinister Abbé Boullan performed sexual rites with the aid of a nun; Mathers, Woodman and Westcott founded the Order of the Golden Dawn; Madame Blavatsky and Colonel Olcott founded the Theosophical Society. Occultism swept from America to Russia in the biggest revival so far.

It is true that interest in the occult is usually a romantic reaction against 'civilisation'; most of the great figures of occultism are *poètes manqués*. In a few cases — Crowley and A.E., for example — the poetry was by no means bad; and this increases our suspicion that magic is basically a form of fantasy, of escape from the boredom of everyday living. But although there is some truth in this, it misses the real point. 'Magic' springs from man's recognition that he possesses powers that are inaccessible to everyday awareness. Man has spent thousands of years learning to master this physical world in which he lives; but in learning to deal with everyday reality, he has also become its slave. It is all very well for Milton to talk about "thoughts that wander through eternity", but most people's thoughts never go much further than next year's Cup Tie or World Series. Like a deep-sea diver, man has put heavy weights on his spirit to hold him on the bottom, and he doesn't know how to take them off.

And yet all intelligent people know that the spirit can soar like a bird. "Every man has an innate inclination to fly," remarked Hoffmann, "and I have known serious, respectable people who in the late evening fill themselves with champagne so as to rise like a balloon." Flying' is obviously a part of human destiny, and this applies to businessmen as well as poets. You only have to set out on a holiday to experience something that can only be described as 'expansion of the senses': your faculties seem to stretch out, as if your nerves had been extended like strands of a spider's web; everything strikes you as fresh and exciting and full of possibilities. And occasionally, these moods of 'expansion' become so intense that they might be described as 'cosmic consciousness'. One of the classic descriptions of such an experience occurs in *The Brothers Karamazov*, where Alyosha walks about into a starry night, and suddenly feels as if there are threads linking his soul with all the stars; he flings himself down, weeping and kissing the earth.

Now the rationalist would dismiss this by saying it is 'just a feeling'. There aren't really threads between Alyosha's soul and the stars. According to this view, mystical experiences have no more objective reality than the pink elephants of an alcoholic. And this is the very root of the argument. For an 'occultist' would reply that there are thousands of authenticated cases of telepathy, second sight, thaumaturgic cures ('miracles'), premonitions of danger or disaster....

Take this example, which can be found in *Doubtful Schoolmaster*, the autobiography of an ex-headmaster, Hugh Heckstall Smith. He was standing by a piano, looking through some music. An Irish girl, sitting nearby, said: 'No, it isn't there'. 'What isn't?' 'What you're looking for—Beethoven's Appassionata.' She was right. I mention this case because Hugh is an old friend; he is a Quaker, not in the least interested in the occult—his real enthusiasm being for mathematical physics. In the same book, he tells a story of his schooldays. His father arrived at his school one day having bought him a cycling cape. His father started to say: "You won't guess where I bought this...." "Don't tell me," said Hugh, "I'll tell you." And he proceeded to describe the small second-hand shop, many miles away. I asked him how he could be so certain. "I don't know. As he spoke, I suddenly got a clear picture of the second-hand shop."

You will observe the jump in my argument—from Alyosha's moment of 'cosmic consciousness' to a case of ordinary telepathy. But this *is* the basic assumption of magic and occultism: that if we could 'free' our senses, at a moment's notice, and allow them to float and stretch out to the stars, we would become 'aware' of all kinds of things that we do not usually know. All animals possess a certain degree of 'psychic powers'—'second sight', the homing instinct, sense of danger. Human beings do not *need* these powers—at least, not very often. In the long course of evolution we have 'retracted our occult faculties, like a snail drawing in its horns'. We *had* to: we had to remain alert and concentrated on the present; we had to learn to do boring things like building houses and digging sewers. But we have now reached a point in evolution where this no longer applies, Western man has too much leisure. Most of his psychological problems today are due to boredom. He needs to 'expand' again, to re-activate the latent faculties.

This is not as difficult as it sounds. To begin with, it requires mainly a kind of relaxation. Here is an example. A couple of years ago, I took my family to Disneyland, near Los Angeles; it is basically a vast amusement park covering many acres. I left them there for the morning, while I went off to lecture at a nearby college. I arrived back around midday, and then remembered I had forgotten to arrange exactly where to meet them. In theory, I could have spent the afternoon wandering through the crowds. Instead, I deliberately relaxed and 'opened' myself, then strolled wherever my feet wanted to take me. Within five minutes, I had found them. If I had remained 'tense', or tried searching systematically, it would probably have taken hours.

This makes another central point. There are other ways of 'opening up': psychedelic drugs will do it; so, to a lesser extent, will alcohol. I suspect that if I had taken LSD, I might have found my family just as effectively. (The only time I have taken a psychedelic—mescalin—I had a strong sense of acquiring powers of second sight and telepathy.) But it would have lasted for the rest of the day, and I shouldn't have been a very good guardian of my children in that state. We need to learn to 'expand' our faculties at a moment's notice, *but also to contract them again*. Cows and dogs do not possess our power of 'contraction'; it has taken us millions of years to acquire it. It would be stupid to throw it away. This is why I have always felt so strongly that drugs are not the answer to the problem of how to expand the senses.

I must try to be more precise about these 'inner powers'. In order to exercise them, it is necessary to use the imagination. A few months ago, I approached an occultist named Robert Leftwich, to ask for information on psychokinesis—the power to move physical objects by the mind alone. He obligingly sent me a kind of paper dart, made by folding a small square of paper across the middle, and also from corner to corner (so the folds look like the crosses on a Union Jack). When the folds are pinched inwards, this makes a paper dart with four fins. Leftwich told me to stick a needle in a cork, and to balance this dart on top of it—so the whole thing looks like a little roundabout. I should then tie a handkerchief across my nose and mouth—so as not to breathe on it—and try to *will* the roundabout to move. Well, I tried it until I was black in the face, and I couldn't make it budge. But I kept it beside my typewriter, and the next day, had another try. This time, to my surprise, it moved. I kept it there for several days, trying whenever I thought of it. Once I had got the knack, it seemed fairly easy to make it move. I would cup my hands around it, stare at one side, and will it to move. After a moment or so, it would start off slowly. Then I would try concentrating on the other side; the thing would come to a stop, then revolve the other way. Being a natural sceptic, I was inclined to suspect that the heat of my hands might have influenced it—like those lampshades in restaurants that turn in the heat of the bulb. Not long afterwards, I mentioned the phenomenon to another student of the occult, Alan Hull Walton, who pointed out that the 'knack' involves using the *imagination* as well as the will. I immediately saw that this seemed to fit my own experience; after the first day, I imagined it turning as well as willing it to turn.

And this brings me to the central problem. The powers of the human imagination are so enormous that they are *dangerous*, like high-voltage electricity. It is just as well that we limit them

19

so much. Think of what happens if you feel sick. If something distracts you—like rain pattering on the windows—you often find that the sickness has vanished. And if you can get the knack, you can learn to dissipate your sickness. It seems to depend on your *attitude*. If you use your imagination positively, not expecting to be sick, you cease to feel sick. If you feel gloomy and distracted, your imagination becomes negative and *amplifies* the nausea. People stutter and get stage-fright for the same reason. The human imagination is an enormous force. If a man can envisage something delightful or desirable, his mind stretches into the future, and he becomes irresistible. As soon as he allows his imagination to become possessed by forebodings or self-pity, his strength ebbs away.

It is amazing that human beings have never recognised this. If you merely lift your hand, or wriggle your fingers, the 'trigger' is imagination. When a great pianist or violinist plays a concerto, the imaginative control is tighter, more precise. And, as Aleister Crowley points out in a passage of his autobiography, 'magic' is basically the use of this same faculty—this confident 'stretching out' of our hidden powers to produce a certain result. Most people, for example, possess the power of the 'evil eye'. Bernard Shaw, who might be assumed to be an arch sceptic, wrote in a letter of 1885: "All the people I ever hated died. A deadly but horrible emanation comes from the hater to his victim." In 1925, he experienced this at first hand. He was making a speech, urging the dramatist Granville Barker to return to the theatre; suddenly he experienced an agonising pain down his back, "as if my spine had become a bar of rusty iron". For precisely a month he was unable to lean forward. Someone later told him that throughout his speech, Granville Barker's wife had been glaring at his back with a look of concentrated fury. I am inclined to believe that anyone with any power of concentration can exercise this power. I am equally certain that anyone who does so deliberately ruins their chance of 'expanding' the senses; for some law of reciprocity says that hatred does equal damage to both parties.

The imagination is dangerous because we do not yet know how to control it. It is rather like carrying a large, flat bowl of water across a room; if you tilt it ever so slightly, the water rushes from one side to the other, and you spill it. Imaginative people have the same trouble. When they are happy, or have something to look forward to, imagination transforms their world into a foretaste of paradise; when they are miserable or frightened, it wrecks their vitality, tears the bottom out of their self-confidence like a ship crashing into rocks. This also explains why psychedelic 'trips' often drive people insane. The mind is opened to a wider range of experience—the great stimulant of imagination. If the imagination is focused on the pleasant aspects, the experience is delightful; but if imagination is negative, the result is 'nausea' magnified many times over.

In short, we possess inner mechanisms that can flood us with ecstasy or plunge us into a horrible sense of meaninglessness. And unlike the simple mechanisms by which we start the washing machine or flush the lavatory, these are at once simple and extremely subtle. This was the subject of Proust's enormous novel: the taste of a biscuit dipped in tea suddenly brings back his childhood as though it were yesterday, but he spends years trying to repeat the trick and even then, only succeeds briefly, by accident, in the twelfth volume. The mind is a vast world in itself; and, like the external world, its 'natural resources' are enormous. The romantic poets caught glimpses of gigantic inner vistas, mountain ranges and oceans; then the clouds covered the scene, and they were again trapped in the boring world of everydayness.

All this is so mysterious that I have become increasingly convinced that the legend of the 'Fall' is basically true. At some time in his remote history, man must have been godlike. Otherwise, how can we explain these powers that he glimpses in flashes? For example, the powers of mathematical prodigies, who, at the age of ten, can multiply together two eighteen-figure numbers *in the head* and produce the answer in half a minute? It is true that these prodigies normally lose their powers as they approach manhood; but they are obviously *there*, lying latent inside them, waiting to be called upon. So is the power that Proust glimpsed—to recall one's *whole* past with total reality, as if it were happening at the moment.

I do not know why man 'fell'. Perhaps just laziness; I define the problem in a novel called *The Man Without a* Shadow* in a single sentence: Human beings are like grandfather clocks driven by watch springs. That is, we have the machinery, but not enough 'electricity' to drive it, any more than you could run an electric fire off a torch battery. We live in a kind of dream or delirium, with only brief glimpses of reality. But we possess the power to 'focus' reality—as Proust did for a moment. That power I have labelled 'Faculty X'.

And how does all this connect up with the kind of magic you will find described in this volume?

All magic springs from man's instinctive recognition that he was once a god, that there is a sleeping superman inside him, if only he could 'raise' it. Otherwise, why would the witches of the past have offered to sell their souls to the devil? Would anyone choose eternal damnation—which they took for granted—unless some strange power inside them stirred and said: 'I am sick of being *merely* human. I want to ride on the wind and conjure storms and feel myself the equal of the lightning.' Magic is an obscure striving towards the realisation of Faculty X. In this volume, you will learn something about its lengthy initiation ceremonies—starting with the necessity to copy out a whole *grimoire* (book of ritual magic) by hand, and sometimes involving months of rigorous preparation. These ceremonies are an attempt to stir the depths of the spirit— you might almost say, to blast them with a depth-charge.

Sometimes, the ceremonies are deliberately disgusting—as can be seen in the Crowley story—because disgust also stirs the depths of the mind. I personally dislike this aspect of Crowley—crucifying cats, and so on—because I feel that it reflects a kind of immaturity, an inability to feel, a juvenile egoism, rather than any real understanding of a basic principle of magic. But there can be no doubt that Crowley was a real magician; he *could* control certain inner powers; and moral judgements must be left to the individual reader.

There are one or two stories in this volume which must be regarded as pure entertainment. I find it difficult to agree with Peter Haining that Arthur Machen, Conan Doyle and Sax Rohmer were real 'occultists', rather than literary men who dabbled in the subject. But their stories are worth reading because they catch something of the atmosphere of the 'occult revival' of the late nineteenth century. Others, I think, deserve to be taken altogether more seriously. Yeats's 'magic' was not all wishful thinking (like the fairyland of his early poems); he definitely understood something about it, something basic, as can be seen from his essay on magic in *Essays and Introductions*. Madame Blavatsky was an old charlatan; but she was another who knew about magic and possessed a high degree of mediumistic powers. (I must emphasise that charlatanism and genuine powers often go together; just as, in Rasputin, charlatanism and religious mysticism went together; magical powers are often *accidental*, something that certain people are born with, and their personality and moral character may be on an altogether lower level.) Dion Fortune was an important and greatly underrated occultist, who was unfortunately born in the wrong half of the century—after the decline of magic; otherwise she would have achieved wider fame; her time is to come. Eliphas Levi was also something of a fake, and his natural powers were weaker than Madame Blavatsky's or Crowley's. (Crowley believed he was a reincarnation of Levi.) But his lifelong obsession with magic led him to understand something of its true nature, and the story of his raising of Apollonius of Tyana could well be more than 50 per cent true. As to Huysmans' description of the Black Mass, this can be taken as largely factual, the kind of thing that really was performed in Paris in the 1880s. It is interesting to note, by the way, that until this volume no full and complete translation of this Black Mass scene existed in English, various details having always been omitted.

But what of such matters as raising the devil, or projecting the astral body (as described in Dion Fortune's story)? How seriously can these be taken?

Several years ago, an American publisher commissioned me to write a book, *The Occult*. I had always been interested in 'magic' but in rather the same way as Yeats: that is, as a symbol of that 'other world' that the romantic poets strive to create. My attitude was basically scientific and sceptical. I suppose it still is. But as I went through the enormous amount of research required, I became increasingly impressed. Science and mathematics convince us by their *universality*; if I read a book on physics or astronomy by a Russian scientist, it sounds exactly like a book on physics or astronomy by an American or English scientist. There are no political or racial differences in this world; it is like an inner country whose landmarks look exactly the same to *all* observers and would probably look the same to a man from Mars. In the world of magic, you expect the divergences to be enormous, because each nation has its own magical traditions, and each individual has his own temperamental peculiarities that determine the direction of his interest. What is so astonishing is that there seems to be so little contradiction or disagreement on fundamental points; the Tibetan Milarepa is likely to say something you remember from some mediaeval alchemist; an Ancient Egyptian description of 'astral travel' corresponds closely to something you found in the war memoirs of a retired general who found himself floating over the battlefield after being blown up by a shell. It soon became apparent to me that certain basic 'psychic' or occult experiences seem to be common to all people at all times. When I started my book, I was inclined to be agnostic about 'life after death' for it seemed to me very likely that even highly trained observers may allow their secret wishes to influence their observation. I ended by concluding that there is as much evidence for life after death as for the existence of the planets. I was also surprised to find that there is so much solid evidence for reincarnation. (Amusingly enough, most 'spiritualists' do not accept this.) I was surprised by the extent to which astrology really works—at least, in the hands of a skilled astrologer. (They are as rare as mediums.) And I was extremely surprised to find that the 'astral body' seems to be more than a myth—for this seems to be an obvious example of superstition: the notion that we possess a 'body' made of finer material than our physical body, which can, under certain circumstances, float away. To put it simply, I had expected to be dealing with masses of old wives' tales, with a small core of inner truth, and I ended by finding that many of the old wives were more truthful than I would have thought possible.

This leads to the final point, the real stumbling block for the rationalist. Anyone who has read Freud or Jung may accept that the mind is a bigger and more mysterious place than our great grandfathers realised; and it seems arguable that the 'magical tradition' has always understood this instinctively. But these powers and forces are *inside* the mind. What about the belief in 'evil' as an external force?

Without wishing to sound too dogmatic—for my interest lies in philosophy rather than occultism—I would say that there appears to be evidence of 'forces' outside us, intelligent forces. Suppose that some highly intelligent savages found a radio set and discovered that it made strange noises when switched on. Their first assumption is that it contains demons. Then some of the cooler-headed suggest that a human being is hidden inside it. And after a much longer interval of time, a few of the more brilliant minds make the suggestion that these strange noises are purely natural forces at work, that these valves and wires are the digestive organs of the radio, which make the same grumbling noises as an empty stomach. This explanation satisfies everyone—no demons, no hidden manikins or elves. But then, one day, they accidentally tune in to a broadcast from a ship. And there can be no doubt that these are real voices issuing from the loudspeaker. How can they understand this phenomenon? The dogmatic rationalists will still assert that the voices were somehow 'natural' like the crackles and whines, while the more superstitious will fall back on the old explanation of demons. And it is hard to see how they can ever hit upon the true explanation unless somebody is kind enough to explain.

In John Keir Cross's Introduction to the Faber volume *Black Magic Stories*, there is an anecdote that may help to make my point. Mr Cross tells how a BBC team once tried summoning the Devil on a Hallowe'en programme broadcast from Scotland. At the end of the programme—in which Mr Cross took part—a magic circle was drawn around the microphone, a mediaeval incantation was read aloud, then everyone tiptoed out of the studio, turning off the lights, but leaving the microphone 'live', just in case the Devil chose to utter a few words. Nothing happened. But when Mr Cross got home to his flat, and was warmly tucked up in bed, his six-month-old son began to scream. They found his face and hands bleeding, and something growling and scrabbling inside the windowsill. They later killed the huge rat that had attacked the child. But they never discovered how it had got into a sealed room, with no fireplace, no hidden rat-holes, or why a rat had come all the way from the docks to a respectable Glasgow suburb. Mr Cross firmly believes—and I am inclined to agree—that the invitation to the Devil was basically responsible. Whether it was the Devil or not, some external force, probably evil, decided to show that such matters were not to be joked about.

The universe is full of forces and energies. Our 'radio set' can tune in to many of these—all the wavelengths of light between red and violet, sounds up to a certain pitch, and so on. Animals can tune in to a wider range—hence the homing instinct, sense of danger, 'second sight'. (Robins may navigate by picking up some electromagnetic vibration from the Milky Way.) But there must be thousands of forms of energy to which we cannot 'tune in', even with instruments (at least, with our present crude instruments). Surrounded by all this, how can we state dogmatically that there are no 'other intelligences' beyond the limited range of our senses? Dr David Foster, a cybernetician, has tried to explain the 'coding' of the genes by assuming that certain high-frequency energies (such as cosmic rays) may be carrying 'coded messages'; he originally called his book on the subject *The Cybernetic Universe*, but ended by deciding to call it boldly *The Intelligent Universe*. Anyone who wants to explore the meeting place of science and occultism should read it.** Whether or not he ends by agreeing with Dr Foster, he should at least come to recognise that it is a kind of madness for human beings to assume that we are the only forms of intelligent consciousness in our universe. This may not 'prove' the existence of ghosts or the Devil, but it may jar us out of the narrow state of mind in which they appear to be an absurdity.

**Notes:**

* Which contains a full-length portrait of Crowley. It is also called *The Sex Diary of Gerard Sorme*.

** For Colin Wilson's introduction to this book: see Appendix. *Ed*

# 3

# Foreword: *The Roots of Witchcraft* (D12)

by Michael Harrison
London: Frederick Muller, 1973.

When Michael Harrison mentioned to me that he was writing a book on witchcraft, I experienced a certain misgiving. I had just completed a large book called *The Occult*, which had involved reading everyone from Margaret Murray and Trevor-Roper to such dubious exponents as the Reverend Montague Summers and Gerald Gardner. The great witch persecutions, which may be said to have ended with the trials of the Salem witches in the last decade of the seventeenth century, began with the Church's persecution of the heresy known as Catharism in Languedoc around the year 1200; the 'witches' rooted out and burned by the Church's inquisitors were actually Cathars. Almost everything that is about those five centuries of persecution can be found in Rossell Hope Robbins's *Encylopedia of Witchcraft and Demonology*. I could hardly see the need for another book on witchcraft. I should have known better. In this book, Michael Harrison makes hardly any references to the five centuries of witch persecution; he is interested in a remoter period. His *Roots of Witchcraft* should rather, I think, be classified with Robert Graves's *The White Goddess*—a poet's investigation into the language and mysteries of a pre-Christian religion.

Michael Harrison mentions the 'origin' of his book on page 43—perhaps it would have been better to do so earlier. He explains that he talked to Professor Geoffrey Webb after the Second World War about some curious discoveries he had made in churches. A bomb had displaced a great stone slab covering the altar of an old church; inside the altar, Professor Webb found a stone *lingam* or phallus. Webb found that 'ninety per cent of all churches examined, of a date up to, say, the Black Death of 1348...had The God (i.e., a ritual phallus) concealed within the altar....' As long ago as 1921, Margaret Murray had suggested, in *The Witch-Cult in Western Europe*, that the 'witches' who were persecuted were actually adherents of a pre-Christian fertility religion—a suggestion that had already been made in the eighteenth century by an Italian, Girolamo Tartarotti. Her book, although found unacceptable by many scholars, is still regarded as a serious work of scholarship. This is not true of her later works, *The God of the Witches* and *The Divine King in England*, the latter of which argues that many kings of England met their deaths in order to fulfil rituals of this ancient religion. At about the time Michael Harrison was learning about the phalluses concealed in Christian altars, my old friend Hugh Ross Williamson was writing a book called *The Arrow and the Sword*, which accepts Margaret Murray's arguments about the 'Old Religion' and contends that King William and Archbishop Thomas à Becket were both 'ritual victims'—a view accepted by Michael Harrison in this book.

So, the basic viewpoint of *The Roots of Witchcraft* is close to that of *The God of the Witches*, *The Arrow and the Sword* and T.C. Lethbridge's *Witches: Investigating an Ancient Religion*; and Michael Harrison makes full acknowledgement of the debt. But Margaret Murray's theories are only used as the basis of one of his typical investigations, the kind of thing, I feel, that Sherlock Holmes might have written for a diversion between more narrowly specialist works like the monograph on tobacco ash or the study of the Motets of Lassus. The amazing variety of information certainly sounds as if it came from Holmes's files: for example, on pages 69-70 we learn from two footnotes that the Egyptians split the granite for the pyramids by drilling small holes in the rock, filling them with water, and allowing the water to freeze by night, and that the actual date of Jesus' birth is May 17, 8 BC, at about 2 in the morning.... I find it almost as much pleasure to read him for the footnotes—and snippets of historical gossip—as for the actual argument of the book, which is absorbing enough. As one would expect from him, there is an enormous amount on ancient Greece and Rome—I can think of no writer since Anatole France who takes such a delight in exploring the classical by-ways and seasoning his work with strange fragments of erudition. But I think it would be fair to say that the originality of the book lies in its linguistic investigations, the attempt to trace the origin of words used in witch's spells. I have no idea whether he has been influenced by Levi-Strauss and the Structuralists—I have no doubt he has read them, as he seems to have read everything—but the method of *The London That Was Rome* and the present book could certainly be described as an attempt at 'an archaeology of knowledge'. I confess that I lack the qualifications to judge his thesis, although I am reasonably certain that there are many points at which Professor Trevor-Roper—and other 'atomist' historians—would accuse him of building castles in the air. No doubt the Namier method—examining every fragment of 'historical evidence' under a microscope—is admirable; but takes so long that the castles never get built. History is too important to be left to historians—to adapt an epigram. Michael Harrison has brought to the writing of this book the qualities that he has spent a lifetime accumulating: the novelist's eye for human behaviour, the poet's love of the past, the journalist's delight in strange stories (like the one about the modem Arab doctor who killed his patient trying to beat a genie out of his body).

In a letter to me, Michael Harrison wrote:

"Where from here? Well, given life and continuing health, I see the possibility of a complete emotional release in the type of writing to which the experiments of forty years have, I now realise, inevitably been leading. My present type of writing gratifies and satisfies, first, that obsessive need to write that I share with every other dedicated writer; desire—now recognised by me as having been evident from earliest childhood—to solve puzzles and to demonstrate the solution's proof; and third, that nostalgia which used, throughout my childhood, boyhood, and, indeed, the first half of my life, to trouble me so deeply—but that I now can convert into the richest material of my creative work."

*The Roots of Witchcraft* seems to me the fullest expression so far of his creative desires; I trust it will be the first of many works in the genre.

# 4

# Foreword: *The Power of the Pendulum* (D25)

by T. C. Lethbridge
London: Routledge & Kegan Paul, 1976

I feel that it is largely my own fault that I missed the pleasure—and profit—of knowing T. C. Lethbridge. He moved to Devon in 1957, the same year that I moved to Cornwall; so, until his death in 1971, we were living within a hundred miles of one another. Moreover, in 1965, I picked up a copy of his book, *Witches: Investigating an Ancient Religion*, and observed opposite the title page that he had written a book called *Ghost and Ghoul*. Two years later, I was commissioned by an American publisher to write a book on 'the occult' and settled down to research the subject. I actually quoted *Witches* in the finished book—the anecdote on p. 15, in which he was led, blindfolded, around the cliffs on Lundy Island, holding a dowsing rod, and accurately detected the position of every one of its buried volcanic dykes. Not long after the book appeared, a correspondent asked me why I didn't contact Lethbridge, since he lived so close; accordingly, I packed up a copy of *The Occult* and sent it to him, together with a letter introducing myself. It was his wife, Mina, who replied, telling me that he had died recently. It was only then, lazily, and belatedly, that I bought a copy of *Ghost and Ghoul*, and realised with astonishment—and chagrin—that here was a completely new and original theory about the nature of ghosts which ought to have been discussed at length in my book. I made a kind of belated apology by dedicating my book *Strange Powers*, to Lethbridge and his wife Mina. Since then, I have read all his books, with a growing sense of frustration at the missed opportunity. Now, in introducing his last book, I can at least pay tribute to a man who seems to me to be one of the most remarkable and original minds in parapsychology.

Curiously enough, this interest developed only after the Lethbridges moved to Branscombe, in Devon. Before that, Lethbridge had spent most of his adult life in Cambridge— where he was Keeper of Anglo-Saxon Antiquities at the University Museum of Archaeology and Ethnology. (It was a purely 'honorary' post, but Lethbridge was glad of the independence; he disliked university 'trade unionism' and the need for academic respectability.) Born in 1901, he came to Cambridge soon after the First World War as a student, and it remained his base for the next thirty-five years or so (with the exception of an eighteen-month break in the mid-1940s, when he and Mina, newly married, tried to become cattle farmers on an island off the west coast of Scotland). His attitude to Cambridge seems to have been ambivalent; he left there in 1944 because he was sick of it but returned because he missed it. By 1957—when *Gogmagog* appeared—the love affair with Cambridge was definitely over; he felt the place was becoming too brash and noisy, and the hostile reception given to *Gogmagog* by archaeological colleagues did nothing to strengthen his attachment. Mina—whose family is from Devon—located Hole House, a fourteenth-century house, with attached cottage, near Branscombe, and felt that this was the place they had always been looking for. She was right; they were exceptionally happy there.

Up to this time, Lethbridge's major works were *Merlin's Island* (1948), *Herdsmen and Hermits* (1950), *The Painted Men* (1954) and *Gogmagog*; there are also a number of smaller works on boats including *Boats and Boatmen* (1952) and *Coastwide Craft* (1952). Nothing is more obvious than that Lethbridge thoroughly enjoyed writing. It was probably fortunate that he came to it so late. He had always been a 'loner', whose twin loves were archaeology and the sea. By the time he was in his mid-forties, this independence of mind was well developed and was expressed in a style that was easy, casual, and personal. *Merlin's Island* begins by explaining that the friends whose help he acknowledges are in no way responsible for the 'damnable heresies' contained in its pages. (I am not sufficiently well versed in Anglo-Saxon history to know what these are.) And in a foreword to *Herdsmen and Hermits*, T. D. Kendrick, Director of the British Museum, comments with a kind of reluctant admiration: "It is here that his opinions, on such subjects, for instance, as the early voyages in northern waters, become almost aggressively memorable, even when one has decided not to believe in them. "This pretty picture may be absolutely incorrect", he remarks cheerfully when talking of the broch people...."

*Gogmagog: The Buried Gods* is the story of Lethbridge's search for a giant figure cut into the turf near Cambridge, and it includes a number of startling theories—such as that Druidism and Brahmanism had a common origin at some time in the remote past. It is possible to understand why it aroused academic hostility. To begin with, a number of references to his friend and colleague Margaret Murray make it clear that he accepts her basic theory, advanced in *The God of the Witches*, that 'witchcraft' is an ancient nature religion based on the worship of the moon goddess Diana. The theory has always had many supporters, and as many bitter opponents, who regard it as little better than imaginative fiction. Margaret Murray enjoyed the dismay she caused; she even enjoyed teasing her academic colleagues until they were speechless with rage. Lethbridge's book concludes that the ancient religion of prehistoric England was the worship of the earth mother, Magog (who is identified with the moon) and her husband Gog, the sun, and his views could be interpreted as powerful support for Margaret Murray's theories of 'wicca'. As I re-read the book, I can see why it would enrage academic historians; what is astonishing is that a member of an academic community—and keeper of a university museum—could write with such breezy independence of mind and such a lack of the usual conditional clauses.

If the attacks hastened Lethbridge's decision to leave Cambridge, then we should thank his hostile colleagues. The independence allowed his mind to return to a subject that had always interested him: the hidden powers of the mind. His mother had been fascinated by the subject of fortune telling and in the days of his first marriage Lethbridge himself had taken an interest in the powers of a clairvoyant who was able to 'see' scenes from the past. Lethbridge had seen a ghost in his undergraduate days at Cambridge—I shall refer to this again in a moment—and had also discovered, at a fairly early stage, that he was a good dowser.

Now, at Branscombe, they made the acquaintance of an elderly lady who was wholly immersed in 'occult' subjects. She talked to them about pendulums, pentagrams and related matters. She was also, apparently, able to 'project her astral body', and wander around and visit her acquaintances at night, as he tells in this present book (and also in The Legend of the Sons of God). Lethbridge apparently tried his skill with a pendulum and discovered that it worked. The pendulum is used in much the same way as the divining rod but can give far more information. Not only will it swing in a circle over some buried object (say, a silver spoon) but can also give precise information on the age of the buried object. It can 'answer questions'—which leads Lethbridge to conclude that it actually serves as some form of contact between a part of the mind that already knows these things, and our limited everyday consciousness. I personally have no doubt whatever that certain minds can perceive all kinds of things that are hidden from the rest of us. I spent two days in Utrecht making a television documentary about the 'paragnost' Gerard Croiset. Like some freak television set, Croiset's mind picks up spontaneous 'pictures' of other times and other places. For example, he might be handed a wrapped parcel connected with an unsolved murder case and say: 'This contains a cigarette box and a potato sack. The box came from the house of one of two brothers who murdered a teenage girl in a cow barn, and the sack was used to wrap her body....' Croiset is also able to 'see' the future; in many cases of drowning, he has been able to say: 'The body will float to the surface next Tuesday morning and in the vicinity of the maritime museum in The Hague...' and has been proved correct. Croiset's everyday consciousness is apparently able to have direct contact with this 'other mind' — perhaps the 'Superconscious' — that knows such things. Lethbridge believes that, for at least one third of mankind (perhaps more), the pendulum can produce the same kind of results, although with less detail.

The experience of using the pendulum, and the sense of freedom from academic restraints, apparently decided Lethbridge to write a book about 'occult' topics. The result was *Ghost and Ghoul*, a book I now heartily wish I had read when it appeared in 1961. In this book, Lethbridge advances the interesting theory that many 'ghosts' — perhaps the majority — are simply a form of 'tape recording'. This line of thought developed from his experience with pendulums. He had established, to his own satisfaction, that material things retain the impress of events in which they have been involved. A sling stone used in a battle two thousand years ago still gives a reading for 'anger' when a 40-inch pendulum is suspended above it. A paragnost like Croiset might well receive actual impressions of the battle as he held the stone. Is it not possible that many 'ghosts' are 'recordings' that are played back accidentally when the right observer comes along? The same thing seems to be true of 'ghouls', or the 'nasty feeling' that can be experienced in certain places. Lethbridge has a fascinating story, dating back to 1924, of a ghoul he encountered in a chorister's school in a cathedral close. He and a friend walked into the spot at the bottom of the stairs and experienced a 'wall of icy cold', imbued with a feeling of misery. When they stepped towards it, the 'ghoul' retreated up the stairs. They followed it step by step up to the roof, wondering if it would suddenly materialise and confront them; instead, it reappeared behind them, and they drove it back downstairs to the hall. This 'ghoul', Lethbridge thought, had been projected from the subconscious mind of some person who was afraid of a ghost that was reputed to haunt the end room in the corridor.

A comparison of *Ghost and Ghoul* and the slightly later *Ghost and Divining Rod* (1963) enables us to see the way in which Lethbridge's theories developed. (The book that came in between these two was *Witches*, but since this deals mainly with Margaret Murray-type theories of witchcraft, it need not concern us here.) In the earlier book, he had described seeing the ghost of a woman of about seventy in a garden near Hole House and advanced the theory that she was a 'projection' of somebody's mind. Now, in *Ghost and Divining Rod*, he draws a further conclusion from something he had already noticed in the earlier book: that an underground stream ran under the lane where he was standing, imparting to the atmosphere above it a 'tingly' feeling. He also mentions a 'ghoul' which both he and his wife experienced on Ladram beach, at a spot where a stream ran into the sea. Could the 'electromagnetic field' of the water be somehow to blame—that same 'field' that produces the response in the dowsing rod? Is it possible that such fields can receive the impress of an emotion, as the sling stone received the impress of anger, and transmit it later to someone who stands on the same spot? He invents the term 'naiad field' for the electromagnetic field of water and advances the suggestion that mountains and open spaces (like deserts) may also have their own individual fields.

Throughout the nine 'occult' books (beginning with *Gogmagog* and ending with the present volume), Lethbridge's thought is always changing and expanding. Sometimes he changes his mind completely; more often, he modifies a theory advanced in an earlier volume. None of the books attempts to present a complete 'system' of ideas; a theme that is only mentioned in one may be developed in another. (For example, the theme of precognition and dreaming is briefly mentioned in *Ghost and Ghoul*, to be fully developed in the present volume.) The final impression is of a brilliant, intuitive intelligence that never ceases to develop.

My own impression is that with the book called *ESP: Beyond Time and Distance* (1965), Lethbridge entered a new phase of his investigation. In the preface, he describes an incident that occurred on one of his early journeys of exploration to Greenland; chasing a wounded bear, he suddenly fell through a hole in the ice and found himself floundering in icy water. Now, he says, something of a similar nature has happened to him again: "I seem to have suddenly fallen through into [a world] where there are more dimensions." I feel that, up to this point, he had thought of himself basically as an archaeologist and naturalist who was pursuing a rather interesting side-line. Now it seems as if he has suddenly recognised that what he is 'on to' may be more important than any of his work as an archaeologist. The books take on a new force and direction; now he experiments non-stop with the pendulum and makes all kind of interesting discoveries. For example, a casual remark by his wife — about why some trees are considered 'unlucky' — led him to try studying various types of wood with the pendulum. Elder — a traditionally unlucky tree — gave a reaction for maleness and repulsion, while rowan — regarded as a protection against magic spells — gave a reaction for femaleness and attraction. One remembers Tolkien's hostile trees in *The Lord of the Rings*, and Robert Graves' long investigations into the ancient tree worship of the Druids. It becomes possible to see what Lethbridge meant by saying he felt as if he had stumbled into another world. Like Graves, he believes that "earlier men knew far more about all this than we know today". But Graves also believed that these early men possessed another kind of knowledge than we possess today. Our knowledge is mostly intellectual, a 'daylight' knowledge, which Graves associates with the sun; there is another kind of intuitive knowledge, a 'lunar' knowledge, symbolised by the White Moon Goddess herself.

This seems to me to be one of the most exciting things about Lethbridge. He is always stumbling on important insights. Sometimes he follows them up; sometimes he merely mentions them in passing. I have heard his books criticised on the grounds that they are repetitive and inconclusive. But this is necessarily so. They are a kind of working journal into which he poured his fresh discoveries and insights year by year; if they are chaotic, they share that fault with the notebooks of Leonardo and the daily journals of every important discoverer. It is fortunate for us that Lethbridge decided to write down his discoveries piecemeal in seven or eight small books, rather than storing them up for some large definitive work; the book might never have been written, and the notes would still be unpublished.

But it was in the next book, *A Step in the Dark*, that Lethbridge first stated what may be his major discovery. In *ESP*, he had noted that the pendulum 'rate' for death seems to be 40 inches, and that dead objects also respond to 20 inches; which led him to speculate that 40 inches may 'represent life force on a higher plane'. All earthly objects, including such ideas as danger and time, have rates between 0 and 40. But by extending the pendulum beyond 40 — the death rate — Lethbridge discovered that the pendulum responds once again — the new length being its 'earthly' rate, plus 40 (i.e., the rate for carbon is 12, and it can also be detected at 52.) But the pendulum now swings over a 'false position' to one side of the object. Lethbridge concludes that there is another realm or dimension in which things also exist — beyond death. Moreover, if the pendulum is extended yet another 40 inches, the same thing happens all over again. But the pendulum gives no rate for 'time' on the second level, as if this realm is somehow timeless; after that, on higher levels, time comes back again. Readers may find this short exposition bewildering, but Lethbridge develops the whole idea further in the present book, and so I can refer them to him.

In short, Lethbridge came to suspect that the pendulum is revealing a realm on the other side of death, perhaps several. Its 'energy rates' seem to be higher than ours, according to the pendulum. Oddly enough, the curious researches of Dr Constantin Raudive on the 'ghost voices' that sometimes appear on magnetic tape seem to point to the same conclusion; these voices seem to be about twice as fast as earthly speech. (Anyone who wants to pursue this point should read Raudive's book *Breakthrough*, and listen to the record that goes with it.) I may also refer to the theories of my friend Dr David Foster, author of *The Intelligent Universe*; Foster is a cybernetician, but has become convinced that the genes of living creatures could only be 'coded' by higher energies than exist on earth—possibly some form of cosmic rays. (I have summarised his idea in the introduction to *The Occult*.) Lethbridge himself was, from the beginning, much preoccupied with this whole problem of Darwinian evolution—with the question: Could living creatures have evolved through a *mechanical* system? His answer—predictably in the negative—is set out most fully in *The Monkey's Tail* (1969), the book that followed *A Step in the Dark*.

If I needed further evidence that Lethbridge possessed intuitive genius of a high order, it would be provided by his last published book, *The Legend of the Sons of God* (which appeared posthumously). In 1968, a German publisher had brought out a book called *Memory of the Future*, which came out in England in 1969 as *Chariots of the Gods?* It made its author, Erich von Däniken, a rich man. But by this time Lethbridge was already at work on *The Legend of the Sons of God*, which looks as if he had read and digested Däniken. (In fact, as he mentions in his preface to *Legend*, he knew nothing of Däniken until a friend sent him the book just as his wife was finishing the typing of *Legend*.) For, like Däniken, Lethbridge is preoccupied with the question of the great stone megaliths like Stonehenge—or the stone circle called the Merry Maidens, in Cornwall. When he tested the Merry Maidens with a pendulum, the reaction was so powerful that the pendulum described a circle that was almost horizontal to the ground. He concluded that some great force is stored in these stones. His arguments led him to the conclusion that the great stone megaliths could have been erected as guides to descending aircraft—a kind of 'landing light'. But if beings landed on our earth as long ago as 2000 BC, then they must have been from another planet, perhaps another galaxy.... Why are there so many legends of 'sons of god' in ancient literature— angels who came down to earth and mated with human beings?

The energy stored in these stones—and probably induced by frenzied religious dances—was probably a form of 'bio-energy', Lethbridge believed. Presumably, the spacemen who visited our earth understood how to utilise this energy. It seems a pity that Lethbridge never came across the interesting ideas of John Michell and his fellow 'ley hunters', who believe that the straight tracks that can be traced on Ordnance Survey maps— ancient bridle paths—joined spots on the earth's surface in which this bio-energy reached a high level—sacred places like Glastonbury and Stonehenge*. I do not know what he would have thought of the theory, but I am convinced that he would have taken it seriously.

This whole subject is too big to be discussed here. Lethbridge would obviously have developed his ideas on the 'sons of god' if he had lived, and he would probably have done so more skilfully and plausibly than Däniken, whose excesses have led many people to dismiss the whole thing as pure fantasy. I myself was inclined to take that view after reading Däniken; it was Lethbridge's book that caused me to change my mind.

I should add that I have also tried dowsing at the Merry

Maidens and, to my amazement, it worked. I say to my amazement because on the only occasion when I had tried dowsing before—in my own back garden—nothing happened, although my wife got a strong reaction. At the Merry Maidens, a friend, Gaston de St Pierre, showed me how to hold the rod; and as I moved beyond the limit of the circle of stones, it shot up until it was almost vertical. Clearly, it was not responding to water, for the 'line of power' runs around the Merry Maidens in a circle, about two feet beyond the stones, and there is unlikely to be a circular underground stream. The centre of the circle also gives a powerful reaction. The day was too windy to try a pendulum; but I am inclined to doubt whether it would work for me. I have tried it in the house, without result. (Again, my wife does it very well.) Lethbridge suggests that people with a strong sexual impulse may be poor at dowsing, and this may explain it; anyone who has read my books will have noted the basic sexual theme that runs through them. As to the matter of the megaliths, I happened to raise this question with the economist E. F. Schumacher shortly after finishing Lethbridge's book. Without prompting, he remarked that he had just returned from an extensive tour of the Middle East, in which he had seen many ancient buildings and tombs with their massive stone blocks, and that he found it inconceivable that the explanation of these blocks could be as simple as the academic archaeologists insist. This was my own feeling when I visited the ruins at Baalbek in 1974 and looked at giant carved blocks that must have taken years to shape and move into place.

I believe that if Lethbridge had lived a year or two longer, he would have become something of a cult figure. (As it is, admirers have raised the idea of starting a Tom Lethbridge Society.) The 'occult revival' began in the early 1960s in France, and by the mid-1960s it had spread all over the world. This may explain why Lethbridge's publishers encouraged him to go on producing an average of a book every eighteen months throughout the 1960s.

Some of the experts believed that the 'craze' would be over by the early 1970s; but at this moment, there is no sign of it; on the contrary, it seems to be gathering momentum. English and American publishers reprint books that have been out of print for seventy years (when the last 'occult revival' ground to a halt), and the paperback houses send out a steady stream of popular books on witchcraft, black magic, astral travel, and astrology. Hardly any of these books have anything new to say, although some of them — like Lyall Watson's *Supernature* — are important summaries of what modern science thinks of the 'paranormal'. Lethbridge's books stand out for their clarity, originality, and sheer literary quality. He was a born writer. He was also the sort of person who would, as he became known to a wider public, have drawn disciples and followers. With a figure like G. K. Chesterton's, he also had some of his personal qualities: kindliness, a child-like humour, and a mind that bubbled with ideas like a glass of champagne. To my mind, these personal qualities emerge most clearly in his unpublished autobiography, one of the most delightful works of its kind I have read since Yeats's. But they can also be found in this present volume — which is, in some ways, one of his most ambitious books. His aim is to review the whole question of whether the world can be described in terms of scientific materialism, or whether something closer to the religious view is correct. Lethbridge is not religious in the ordinary sense — his wife seemed to think he was probably an agnostic. But a man who believes he has accidentally stumbled on a way of establishing that there are other realms of reality beyond this one, and that the 'soul' is probably immortal, has more in common with the religious man than with the sceptic. In fact, Lethbridge was inclined to believe that such distinctions are unnecessary. "What is magic today will be science tomorrow", he says in one of his books. And this remark could be quoted on the title page of all his books; it catches their essential spirit.

One of these days some enterprising publisher will gather together all Tom Lethbridge's 'occult' books between two covers—it would not be unmanageably large. When that happens, I think we shall recognise that he is a classic: not just of parapsychology, but of English Literature.

**Notes:**

* See Chapter 8. *Ed.*

# 5

# Introduction: *An Occultist's Travels* (D22)

by Willy Reichel
Philadelphia: Running Press, 1975

This book is a record of one of the strangest epochs in the history of the human spirit. It is also a fragment of an immense, unsolved mystery story.

That mystery story began on March 31, 1848, when loud rapping noises echoed through the house of the Fox family in Arcadia, New York. Mrs Fox, understandably upset, invited neighbours in to hear the strange noises, which only occurred when her two daughters, ages twelve and fifteen, were present. It was assumed that this was a straightforward case of haunting, and the basement was actually dug up in search for the bones of a peddler who was supposed to have been murdered there. Searchers did in fact find a decomposed body, but the odd thing is that the rapping noises continued to follow the Fox sisters around. That certainly eliminated the haunting theory.

Undoubtedly, all this amounted to what we would now call the poltergeist phenomenon. The Fox case created an absolute sensation; people all over America found that they also could 'communicate' with 'spirits' by means of rapping noises. Then two brothers named Davenport discovered that there was an even more interesting method of contacting the spirits. They would go into a trance, and spirits would take up musical instruments and play them in the dark. These trance subjects soon became known as 'mediums,' and the spirits of the dead not only came and spoke through their mouths, but also manifested themselves in other ways—even materializing in the room and holding discussions with their still-living relatives!

What we must grasp is that until the mid-19th century, such things were virtually unknown. Certainly there had been plenty of ghosts and poltergeists ever since Roman times. For example, in the time of the first Queen Elizabeth, the alchemist Dr John Dee had hired a series of young men gifted with 'psychic powers'—such as second-sight, telepathy, etc. Dee called these young men 'scryers' (meaning 'descryers', or 'see-ers'). The most notable scryer was an Irish ex-criminal named Edward Kelly, who gazed into a crystal ball, went into a trance, and held long conversations with 'spirits' whom Dee believed to be angels. Kelley's spirits were almost certainly the same kind of spirits that the Davenport brothers contacted almost three centuries later; Kelley was a 'medium'—but no one knew it. In the mid-18th century, a retired Swedish engineer named Emanuel Swedenborg found that he had an ability to go into a trance, during which he apparently visited heaven and hell. What Swedenborg, Kelley, and many others had in common was that despite their mediumistic abilities, they apparently were unable to convey spirit messages through their mouths.

All this changed almost overnight in the mid-19th century, an era which we could safely call a 'psychic explosion.' Spiritualist writers announced portentously that a new age had dawned, as world-shaking as Christianity. According to them, God had chosen Jesus Christ as his messenger to the human race, but now (or so it seemed) he had decided to try direct communication, permitting spirits of the dead to return to earth. All this had an absolutely staggering impact upon our great-great-grandparents, to a degree that we can today scarcely imagine. Perhaps we can get some idea if we imagine a saucer-like spacecraft landing at the United Nations Plaza in New York City, piloted by little green men announcing that they have travelled from the Andromeda constellation.

We can get an idea about turn-of-the-century spiritualism from this remarkable book by Willy Reichel, a German professor of 'mesmerism' with considerable healing powers. *An Occultist's Travels* describes, quite simply, Reichel's travels from New York to Japan in the early years of the present century, and the things he saw and heard: America was, at that time, apparently bursting with gifted mediums and fortune tellers, and Reichel's account leads one to believe that many of them were genuine. (He claims that one palmist had foretold the 1906 San Francisco earthquake in an article published by a local newspaper, well in advance of the disaster, which should be easy enough to verify.)

In Chapter Three, you will find a statement that puts the finger on the central problem of all this spiritualistic activity. Reichel comments on the information that 'spirits' have given the living about life after death, adding a warning that, in spite of the convincing nature of so many communications, "the relative value of these statements...is to be accepted very critically, since, according to experience, they contradict themselves with different mediums...." In other words, spirit messages were far from infallible. Because it all tended to be confused and self-contradictory, one might speculate that if there really were spirits, they might have been deliberately giving sceptics an excuse for dismissing the whole spirit phenomena as hysteria.

This raises another interesting point. That period was then the era when hysteria was the commonest emotional disorder. Hysteria has almost disappeared today, having been replaced by other mental illnesses. Significantly 'spiritualist' activity has also diminished. Modern spiritualists themselves admit that the age of 'great' mediums seems to be over.

Why? What precisely happened? Read this book and ask yourself those questions. If all Reichel says is true, then spiritualism is very important. It should have forced science to completely reverse its foundations. Instead, for the most part, scientists sat tight and insisted that the occult explosion was all a lot of nonsense and would soon blow over. And history proved them more right than wrong.

I have no tidy explanation to offer except the obvious one. While I am not a dedicated spiritualist, I am inclined to accept the notion of some sort of 'life after death' rather than not. But I also suspect that what man really discovered in the mid-19th century were the strange forces produced by his own subconscious—or *super*conscious—mind. Before we can even begin to grasp what happened, we may need a completely new picture of nature. We may have to accept, for example, that just as there is a 'luminiferous ether' that conducts electromagnetic vibrations, so there is another kind of ether that conducts mental vibrations.

If Cleve Backster's experiments are correct when they indicate that plants can sense our thoughts, then perhaps we are *all* in contact through this mysterious jelly-like medium, although man's highly developed conscious intellect apparently cuts him off from most of the 'vibrations'. Cats can see in the dark; perhaps plants can 'see' in this psychic darkness, in which the rest of us are blind. But the unconscious—or superconscious —mind may be in contact with this darkness and can produce effects on it; hence poltergeist activities, telepathy, second-sight and the rest.

Twenty years ago, a majority of readers would have dismissed Willy Reichel's book as a collection of inexplicable absurdities. Now, I think, we are at last ready to take it seriously.

# 6

## Introduction: *To Anger the Devil: the Reverend Dr Donald Omand, Exorcist Extraordinary* (D31)

by Marc Alexander
Sudbury, Suffolk: Neville Spearman, 1978.

When my producer at Westward Television told me he wanted me to interview an exorcist, I experienced strong misgivings. It was not that I was afraid he might be surrounded by a smell of fire and brimstone; that would have been intriguing and might have made excellent television. No, what bothered me was that he would probably prove to be a total disappointment, one of those bleating clergymen with university accents who inspire a kind of embarrassed disbelief.

Within minutes of meeting Donald Omand, I knew I didn't have to worry. He was obviously a quiet, gentle soul, whose manner struck me as rather vague; yet he talked about his experiences of the supernatural with a simplicity and openness that showed that he knew what he was talking about. And on the programme itself, there was the same charming matter-of-factness; no theological pronouncements about good and evil, only a down-to-earth acceptance that reminded me of a doctor's attitude towards germs. Whatever else Donald Omand might be, he was not a charlatan.

And what exactly was he? I had skipped through his book *Experiences of a Present Day Exorcist* on the evening before the programme, and found it hard to make up my mind. It was not that I was a sceptic about 'the supernatural'. I had just finished writing an enormous book called *The Occult,* and the study of hundreds of case histories left me in no doubt that there are many things in heaven and earth that most of us never encounter. My own maternal grandfather had once slept in a room with a poltergeist that kept pulling the blankets off the bed, no matter how tightly he wrapped them around him. My grandmother had had premonitions of disaster in the form of a shadowy figure standing by the bed in the middle of the night. But in the majority of cases, 'supernatural' experiences can be explained in terms of the human mind itself—for example, we know that poltergeists are usually associated with a disturbed child or teenager, whose unconscious aggressions and frustrations cause the phenomena.*

Now in the second chapter of his *Experiences,* Donald has a story of how, when he was working with a circus in Germany, the strong man was somehow 'possessed' by an evil spirit as he walked past a group of people holding a black mass on the cathedral steps; this same 'spirit' later passed into the body of a lion, which tore the lion-tamer to pieces. Donald went into the ring and performed his first exorcism, experiencing, as he did so, a curious sense of peace and security. The lions became calm and walked back through the tunnel to their cages. Donald had no doubt whatever that he was dealing with an evil spirit or spirits, not just with human evil.

Although I found this hard to accept, I gradually came to understand why he himself regards it as self-evident. A few weeks later he came down to stay with us at our home near Mevagissey, and we had the chance to talk about his experiences at length. He told me then of how he had inherited 'second sight' from his mother, and how it had somehow been nurtured or developed by a maidservant from the Isle of Skye named Maggie. Many years later, when he was staying in an Iron Curtain country, Maggie appeared to him in a dream and told him to go home at once. He left the next day, and within hours, the secret police had descended on his host and hostess and grilled them about their visitor. If it hadn't been for Maggie's warning, Donald Omand might have spent uncomfortable days or weeks in a communist gaol. But in this case, we can say that it was simply a question of a premonition. And the same thing applies to another of his stories about Maggie: how, as a child, she used to tell him legends of the Hebrides in instalments, and Donald, in turn, repeated these to his brother Campbell. But one day, when he had finished telling Campbell the latest instalment, Donald experienced an absolute certainty about what came next, and went on and finished the story. He is convinced that this was not simply a matter of 'guessing' the ending; it involved a very *precise* knowledge of a legend he had never heard before. But here we can call upon the hypothesis of telepathy. Like most Highland storytellers, Maggie probably knew it by heart and told it always in the same words; Donald had somehow gained access to her 'memory bank'.

There is another type of experience that is exhaustively documented, and that gives us a better insight into the world of Donald Omand's beliefs. I am speaking of so-called 'out of the body experiences', in which people in moments of stress find themselves floating above the physical body, often slightly behind it and to the left. This has been reported so frequently that there can be no doubt that it is a common human experience. That, of course, proves nothing: it could be simply a common delusion, like our dreams of flying. There *are* a few well authenticated cases in which people have reported accurately on things seen while 'outside the body' and been able to verify these impressions later; but these are so rare that no one can blame sceptics who point out that two swallows don't make a summer.

But whether or not these 'out of the body experiences' are what they seem to be, they provide one interesting piece of support for Donald Omand's views. Again, and again, 'astral travellers' have reported encounters with malevolent entities in this twilight realm beyond the body. Oliver Fox—the author of the classic *Astral Projection*, writes: "I caught sight of a hideous monster—a vague, white, filmy, formless thing, spreading out in queer patches and snake-like protuberances. It had two enormous round eyes, like globes, filled with pale-blue fire, each about six or seven inches in diameter...." In my book *Mysteries* I compare this frightening vision with the one experienced by Henry James senior in a cottage at Windsor (an account I had earlier quoted in *The Outsider* in the chapter about evil). James was fully awake, and not 'outside his body', but the vision of evil that brought him close to total breakdown was very like the monster described by Oliver Fox.

It is natural that most people should feel intense scepticism about such things. Fortunately, they are as unlikely to encounter any such terrifying denizens of the 'astral' realm as they are to meet up with a giant octopus—or the Loch Ness Monster. Yet the sheer number of descriptions of such encounters convinces me that they are unlikely to be pure imagination. And this, again, raises the disturbing possibility that 'evil' may not be a purely relative term, another name for malicious stupidity, but may have some kind of independent existence. I have, for example, an account by a man whose word I can trust of how he was about to enter a lock-up garage when he was suddenly paralysed by a conviction that something evil was waiting inside. He tried to tell himself that it was imagination, but his hand simply declined to open the door. And then, quite suddenly, it went away; he opened the door and—as he expected—found everything as usual. And what if he had opened the door earlier? I think he would have seen nothing, but what he *felt* might well have caused a mental breakdown like that described by Henry James senior.

Now the late T. C. Lethbridge, one of the most brilliant amateur parapsychologists of this century, had a convincing explanation of certain phenomena of this type. He called them 'ghouls', and believed they were some odd kind of 'tape recording' of an unpleasant emotion. As a child, he and his mother experienced a highly unpleasant sensation in a wood; they discovered later that the body of a gamekeeper who had committed suicide lay behind some bushes. The man's fear and misery, Lethbridge believes, somehow 'imprinted' themselves on the place—perhaps on some electrical field associated with living trees—and he and his mother experienced it as a physical sensation. In books like *Ghost and Ghoul*, Lethbridge offers many similar examples, and the total effect is very convincing. He believes that the majority of 'ghosts' are also 'recordings' of the same kind. **

Clearly, Donald Omand would not be able to endorse this view. Like all exorcists—indeed, like all Christians—he believes that living powers of evil have an objective existence. For myself, I prefer to keep an open mind. I am inclined to believe that certain 'entities' can exist in a disembodied state. Whether these have anything to do with the Devil is a different matter. It is conceivable that they are the natural inhabitants of some non-physical realm, just as sharks and squids are inhabitants of the sea. Perhaps they exist inside the mind—not as 'imaginings', but as real creatures with an independent existence—a hypothesis I suggested in *The Mind Parasites*. †

In one important respect, Donald Omand's experiences seem to support the 'naturalistic' theory. If these sinister forces were the devils of Christian theology, then any clergyman ought to be able to exercise the power of banishment, provided he used the correct ritual. But this is not so. Donald's ability to perform exorcism is, as he agrees, related to his 'feyness '—the second sight he inherited from his mother. That is to say, he seems to exercise his powers in the same realm of 'spirits' that the Society for Psychical Research has spent so many years investigating, not in the realms of theological good and evil. Donald Omand is undoubtedly a good man, and this no doubt plays a part in his ability to perform exorcism; but there are probably thousands of clergymen who are just as kindly, benevolent and charitable as Donald who possess not the slightest vestige of the power to perform exorcism. And I have no doubt that the majority of the saints would also have been ineffective.

And why do I take the trouble to emphasise this point? Not, I assure you, out of any desire to minimise the importance of his work. Yet I suspect that many of the readers of this book— and of those who read it in its newspaper serialisation—may feel that they are being asked to swallow something they find slightly incredible: not that Donald Omand can perform effective exorcisms, but that what he is doing somehow 'proves' the Christian doctrine of evil angels and minions of the Devil. It *may*; but then, my own view is that there is nothing in this book that could not be accepted by an atheist or an agnostic; or, for that matter, by a thoroughly sceptical psychoanalyst. In my own view, the religious question is irrelevant. The main thing we have to decide—every one of us for ourselves—is whether Donald Omand is simply a kind of psychologist who can heal sick minds, or whether he has power over certain non-human entities that *can* cause trouble to human beings. If the latter is true—as I believe—then we have answered one question only to create a hundred more. But then, this need hardly disturb us since it is the way that new fields of knowledge are opened, and new sciences come into existence.

Notes:
* Colin Wilson later changed his mind about this explanation of poltergeist activity (see Chapter 12). *Ed.*
** See Chapter 4. *Ed.*
† Colin Wilson's science fiction novel, first published in 1967, recently reprinted by Monkfish Book Publishing with an Introduction by Gary Lachman.

# 7

# Foreword: *Ritual Magic: an occult primer* (D29)

by David Conway
New York: E. P. Dutton, 1978.
New edition as *Magic: an occult primer* by Witches Almanac
Inc., 2016.

This strikes me as one of the best books on magic that has been written in the twentieth century, and one of the best introductions to magic (an altogether rarer phenomenon), written in any century. I have only one minor criticism. The author is a genuine magician; consequently, he fails to grasp the extent to which the rest of us find the whole idea of magic frankly absurd. Let me see if I can make the proposition sound any less illogical.

In August 1888, a young man named Charles Johnston was sitting in the room of Helena Petrovna Blavatsky, the founder of Theosophy. Madame Blavatsky was playing patience; her friend Colonel Olcott, on a visit to her, was writing a letter at a side table; Johnston was sitting nearby, carrying on a desultory conversation with both. Madame Blavatsky became impatient as the cards refused to 'come out'; she frowned and drummed her fingers on the tabletop. Then, quite unconsciously, she raised her hand well above the table, continuing to drum with her fingers. The tapping sounds on the table continued. Realizing that Johnston was watching her with interest, she turned towards him and began to tap on the back of his hand—without rising from her seat. He was five or six feet away from her. Now amused by her game, she transferred the taps to the top of his head. Johnston writes: "I could both feel and hear them. It was something like taking sparks from the prime conductor of an electric machine; or better still perhaps, it was like spurting quicksilver...."

Johnston goes on to say that this was "A quite undoubted miracle." It was, of course, nothing of the sort. It was a perfectly ordinary phenomenon which has been observed hundreds— probably thousands—of times by psychic researchers. It is known as a 'poltergeist effect'. Madame Blavatsky was particularly good at it; when she first met her disciple, Sinnett, he told her that he had tried spiritualism, but could not even get the spirits to rap on a table. "Raps are the easiest to get," said Madame Blavatsky, and made raps sound from all over the room. A vagabond named William Drury had made the same discovery two hundred years earlier; he was arrested at the small town of Ludgershall, in Wiltshire, in 1661; his drum was confiscated, and he was sent to jail. Immediately afterwards, the house of the magistrate who had sentenced him was disturbed by loud drumming noises, which went on every night, together with other strange phenomena. The case—known as 'the phantom drummer of Tedworth'—is attested by dozens of witnesses. Drury admitted to a visitor that it was he who was somehow causing the disturbances, and when he was transported out of the country, they ceased.

Perhaps the most amazing and convincing case is one that has been published since Mr Conway first wrote this book. In the early 1970s, the Toronto Society for Psychical Research, under the direction of Dr George Owen and his wife Iris, decided to try to create a ghost. A group of researchers invented the life story of a seventeenth century cavalier called Philip, who had a tragic love affair with a gypsy girl and committed suicide. They then sat around and tried to persuade the imaginary ghost to rap on a table. For months, nothing happened, although they tried hard. Then, one day when they had *stopped* trying, loud raps began to sound from the table. The 'spirit' identified itself as Philip and told his life story in detail; it also made the table waltz around the room. Philip eventually became such a professional performer that he even made the table levitate in front of a television audience.

In short, there can be no reasonable room for doubt that 'poltergeist effects' originate in the human subconscious mind— more often than not in the minds of disturbed adolescents. Yet we do not have the slightest idea of *how* the mind can cause an object to fly through the air or make rapping noises all over the room. What energies are involved? How do they work? At the moment, no one has even managed to offer a convincing explanation.

Now I would submit that this is what is usually meant by 'magic'. It is true that the legendary 'great magicians'—from Merlin to Gandalf—could do far more spectacular things; Merlin is supposed to have transported the great trilithons of Stonehenge from Ireland by magic. (He didn't—they were there two thousand years before King Arthur's time). But if you read any book about the history of men who were supposed to be able to perform magic, from Apollonious of Tyana to Aleister Crowley, you will discover that their feats were far less spectacular. Crowley once demonstrated his powers to an acquaintance in New York; he fell into step behind a respectable looking gentleman, imitating his walk exactly. Suddenly, Crowley allowed himself to crumple at the knees; the man in front of him also fell on to the pavement; he got up looking puzzled and frightened, wondering what had happened.

And now, I think, my own basic theory of magic should be emerging. 'Magical powers' originate in the unconscious mind. And the reason that we are very naturally sceptical about their existence is that what you call 'you' and I call 'me' is our conscious egos. Disturbed adolescents can cause 'poltergeist effects' because their unconscious minds are far more highly charged than the average person's by tensions due to physical changes. (For the same odd reason, menstruating women can

57

sometimes produce the same effects—a fact that is recognised by most primitive tribes). In most of us, the unconscious has adjusted itself to the routine of everyday life and sees no good reason to make unusual efforts. So it yawns and relaxes. A man like Crowley deliberately kept his 'unconscious' supercharged by practising strange magical rituals and by behaving in a way that would strike most of us as deplorable. (For example, he filed his teeth so as to be able to draw blood from his girlfriends, who were usually masochists).

Now all this sounds incredible enough. But in the past two or three years, there has emerged at least one piece of scientific evidence whose value seems to me incalculable. I am speaking of the discoveries made by R. W. Sperry and others in the field called 'split brain research'. What they have discovered, basically, is that there are *two* people living inside our heads. The right and left sides of our brains have quite different functions— this has been known for more than a century. The left deals with language, with ideas, with analysis; the right with recognition, with intuition. In other words, to put it crudely, the left is a scientist, and the right is an artist. But the two halves are joined by a knot of nerve fibre which keeps them in close contact, like the hot line between two neighbouring states. If this fibre is separated (as it sometimes is to cure epilepsy), the results can be rather odd. If the left eye is shown an apple, and the right eye is shown an orange, and the person is *asked* what he has just seen, he replies: 'An orange'. But if he is asked to *write* what he has seen with his left hand, he writes 'apple'. If asked what he has just written, he will reply: 'orange'. (It should be mentioned that, for some reason, the right hemisphere of the brain governs the left side of the body, and vice versa). Moreover, if the right side of the brain is shown an obscene picture, the patient will blush; asked why he is blushing, he replies: 'I don't know'. And he doesn't. In other words, the person who calls himself 'I' is actually only the left side of the brain: sitting only a few centimetres away there is another 'you', who exists as a completely independent person. The right hemisphere is silent; yet it is just as much an individual as the left.

This explains, at least, how it is possible for a person to cause poltergeist effects and yet be totally unaware that he is the cause. (This is so almost invariably—Dr Owen warns psychical researchers against telling young people who are the focus of such disturbances that they are to blame; it can cause severe shock.) The left is genuinely ignorant of what the right is up to.

The inference would seem to be that the left side of our brain is what Freud called the 'ego'; the right is, presumably, what he called the 'id', or the unconscious. Or, at least, is the gateway to the unconscious. For there are other mysterious 'lower regions' of the brain—the cerebellum, the limbic system, the 'reptile brain', a relic of our remote past in primeval seas. The psychologist Stan Gooch is convinced that it is the cerebellum—the so-called 'old brain'—that is responsible for 'paranormal experience'. We know almost nothing about the brain. Meanwhile, the experts—like Sperry, Robert Ornstein, Sir John Eccles—are not too happy when amateurs like me begin to evolve curious theories, pointing out that some new discovery tomorrow may change everything. I take their point but—forgive me—decline to stop speculating.

And in the present case, it is easy to see why. These discoveries could be the great breakthrough in the field of paranormal research. Moreover, they suggest all kinds of revolutionary experiments. For example, in the last century, when hypnosis had only recently been discovered, there were many experiments to try to determine whether it could endow people with paranormal powers. There is an immense amount of evidence that it could—certain hypnotized subjects were able to display 'travelling clairvoyance' and describe places that they had never visited. (All this can be found in the four volumes of E. J. Dingwell's classic *Abnormal Hypnotic Phenomena*). But this new knowledge of the functions of the left and right hemispheres suggests that when a person is hypnotized, it is only the left side of the brain that is put to sleep; the right remains as active as ever. (This, at any rate, is my own conviction). And if, as we suspect, the right brain lies at the root of paranormal phenomena, then it might be possible to train it to make more deliberate use of its powers through hypnosis. Another obvious possibility is to attempt to train people who have had the 'split brain' operation, which might be even more rewarding....

Any good book on psychical research will tell you that 'poltergeist effects' are not the only 'strange powers' at the command of certain human beings. There are, for example, many well-authenticated examples of genuine glimpses of the future. This taxes our credulity far more than poltergeist phenomena, because it seems to contradict the recognition that the future has not yet happened. Then there is a vast amount of evidence for the phenomenon known as 'out of the body experience'— people at certain moments find themselves apparently hovering outside their own bodies. The majority of these are not remotely interested in 'occultism'; they are perfectly ordinary people who have had just one single abnormal experience. (It happened to the biologist Lyall Watson, for example, when his Land Rover overturned in Africa; in his 'out of the body' state he saw the position of one of the passengers, halfway through the roof. He recovered consciousness moments later and verified that his observation had been correct.) The evidence for telepathy and 'second sight' is also impressive.

Now all this is, I would argue, a form of what our ancestors called 'magic'. We do not think of such things as magic because the word conjures up Merlin and Dr Faust and Gandalf. This is a mistake, and it explains the understandable and universal scepticism about magic. If, in fact, we can accept that 'paranormal phenomena' are somehow produced by that 'other self' inside the brain, then we have acknowledged that every one of us contains a magician.

At which point, I have to acknowledge that this is not all there is to it. Anyone who has been more than half convinced by my arguments so far may find the second part harder to swallow. I do myself, and I have to admit that I am by no means totally convinced about it.

Let me begin by speaking of a subject that most of us know at least a little about: astrology. Few people can resist surreptitiously reading their horoscope in the daily newspaper, even if they insist—quite truthfully—that they regard the whole thing as a joke.

I agree with the sceptics. Of course astrology is a joke. Of course it is preposterous to suppose that the position of the stars and planets could exert the slightest influence on the life of human beings.... Having said which, I have to shamefacedly admit that, in many cases, it really seems to work. I am willing to agree that it could all be coincidence; yet it *does* seem true that many people born under Cancer are home-lovers with an over-developed protective streak; that Geminis tend to be clever and changeable; that Capricorns are plodders; that Leos are show-offs; that Virgos are precise and tidy; that Pisces are romantics; that Aquarians are detached but kindly; that Scorpios have powerful and often violent emotions.... Moreover, people also display characteristics of their rising sign—the sign that was coming up over the horizon at the moment of their birth. This was investigated by two French statisticians, the Gauquelins, who convinced themselves that this was more than coincidence. They turned over their result to a thoroughly tough-minded psychologist named H. J. Eysenck, who was convinced that the whole thing was nonsense, and that it would only take him a few hours to prove it. Eysenck has ended up by publicly acknowledging that, for some totally unknown reason, people *are* influenced by their rising sign.

In short, it is one of the basic principles of traditional magic that, in some unknown way, there is a link between man and the heavens. 'As above, so below,' said Thrice Great Hermes. It may be some purely mechanical link, as mechanical as the genes that determine the colour of our eyes. One student of astrology, the late Rodney Collin, suggested that when a person is born, something inside him responds like a light meter to the precise configuration of the planets (and, of course, to their gravitational forces). So, each of us is stamped at the moment of our birth like a branded cow. My own theory, for what it is worth, is that the major influence on human beings is the earth itself, which exerts all kinds of strange forces on our minds and emotions. But the delicately balanced magnetic forces of the earth change from moment to moment, as the tides are influenced by the moon. If I am correct, then we are more closely connected to the earth than we realize.

Which brings me to the oddest part. It is only in recent centuries that we have learned about the relation of the heavens to the earth, of the way in which the moon influences the tides and sunspots influence the growth of plants and trees. Yet our ancestors of three thousand years ago had already worked out an elaborate science of man's relation to the universe. If Professors Alexander Thom and Gerald Hawkins are correct, the earliest part of Stonehenge, constructed five thousand years ago, is an elaborate computer for working out eclipses of the sun and moon. We not only have no idea how our Neolithic ancestors acquired such knowledge, but *why* they acquired it. My guess—and in an introduction like this I lack the space to justify it—is that they had a thorough but *instinctive* (i.e., right brain) knowledge of such matters; they knew about the relation between heaven and earth 'in their bones'.

Now it is important to realize that ancient 'magic' is not merely a collection of absurd superstitions—although it inevitably contains plenty of these—but an elaborate knowledge system, as precise and complex as our tables of atomic weights.

Like most people, I had always assumed that it was something
of a joke, until I was asked to write a book on 'the occult'.
What surprised me as I read about Babylonian and Assyrian
and Egyptian and Greek and Roman and Celtic magic was that
they were so incredibly similar. If magic was merely crude pre-
scientific thinking, you would expect the magic of the Eskimos
to differ as much from that of the Central Africans as their
climate; and you would certainly expect to find no resemblance
whatever between the magic of the Norsemen and the ancient
Chinese. This is not so; not only are there dozens of similarities,
there is an obvious basic identity. They were talking about
the same thing. Jungians might explain this by saying that the
human race possesses a collective unconscious—which could be
stretched to mean that both Chinese and African alcoholics will
see pink elephants, and that this proves nothing. Yet it seems
to me more accurate to say that all primitive 'shamans' (or
witch doctors) were trying to describe something they saw in
the *outside* world—an underlying 'order of nature'. This, at any
rate, is my own impression.

This notion that there is some kind of connection between
the universe and man—the macrocosm and the microcosm—is
the basic principle of all magic; it is called a 'correspondence'.
And, according to the ancients, there was not only a system of
correspondences between man and the planets (the stars do not
really count in astrology, being merely the equivalent of the
figures around the edge of a clock), but between the planets and
various animals, colours, scents, gods and so on. And perhaps
most important, between the planets and the various sephira
(or emanations—wishes made manifest) of the Kabbala. The
system of Jewish mysticism known as the Kabbala is the basis
of western magic, its atomic table of the elements, so to speak.
It is such an incredible and fascinating study that I am tempted
to devote a few paragraphs to it here; but Mr Conway has
explained it all so well in the book that it would be pointless.

Anyone who is curious about my own views can find them in my book *The Occult*.

I have to admit that when I first opened David Conway's book on magic—it was sent to me for review by its English publisher—I was inclined to feel dismissive. A history of magic would have been respectable enough, but a book that professes to teach students how to perform simple magic seemed altogether too much of a gimmick. But as soon as I began to read, I was impressed by a certain quality of the author's mind—a sense of genuineness. When I had finished the book, I realized that it *is* a good general introduction to the subject of magic, the kind of thing that would serve a student of anthropology who was writing a paper on the subject. And since the author believes that magic really works, it is only common sense that he should try to offer some basic rules and procedures.

Who is David Conway? The name is, in fact, a pseudonym. Soon after I reviewed the book, we had some correspondence, and he explained that his reason for using the alias was that he was working for the government, and his colleagues in the department might look at him a little oddly if they knew he was a magician. Since then, he has left government service and gone to live in Germany. And now, knowing a little more of him, I realize that it was not entirely because of his government job that he preferred to keep his identity a secret. For there is nothing of the phoney or exhibitionist about David Conway. He is not merely a magician, but a genuine mystic, an intensely private person who is absorbed in what Blake called 'the inner worlds' and their mystery.

This became clear to me when I asked him for some personal details. He is, to begin with, a Welshman—that is, a Celt. For some odd reason, the Celts are the most 'mystical' race on earth. They include, of course, the Irish, the Welsh and the Scots, and certain tribes of Spain. 'Second sight' is common among them. David Conway's experiences of the occult began as a baby, when two strange old ladies used to come to his bedside and talk to him. They also tickled him, and his parents would rush in, wondering why he was shouting. When he told them about the old ladies they took it for granted that he was dreaming, although they were struck with the exactness of his descriptions of the women—he even knew their pet names—(they told him to call them Auntie). Then one day, the local doctor called, and the five-year-old boy described the old ladies. After that, his parents moved him to another bedroom, and he saw no more of them. It was only years later that his parents told him that the old ladies had once lived in the house—forty years earlier. One had died in the bedroom: the other had committed suicide there some three months later.

David Conway's explanation of this curious episode is that the old ladies had somehow left 'memory traces' of their presence imprinted on the room, and the small boy's unconscious mind had picked up these traces when he was relaxed, on the point of sleep, and had 'translated' them into real people. The 'memory trace' theory of 'ghosts' is fairly well-known in psychic circles— it was first suggested by Sir Oliver Lodge around the turn of the century—and is to my mind highly plausible. But in this case, I do not feel that it fits. I get the feeling that Mr Conway is leaning over backwards to try to sound logical when it might be better to acknowledge that this is one of those matters that, at the moment, we cannot even begin to explain.

In order to understand David Conway, it is necessary to accept that there are certain human beings who, from their earliest days, have a strong sense that the solid physical world is only half the story, and that hidden behind it there is a world of 'invisible' reality. William Blake was such a person; so was Emanuel Swedenborg; so was Rudolf Steiner; so was George Russell, better known as the poet AE. All had what would be termed 'supernatural' experiences in childhood; yet all were far more interested in what they felt to be this perfectly natural world concealed behind the visible world of solid objects. It is also worth noting that Blake, Swedenborg, Steiner and Russell were all basically realists, hard-headed men with a definite scientific or practical bent. The same is true of David Conway, as the first chapter of this book shows.

Conway was brought up in a remote country district of Wales. Anyone who knows such areas—I live in a similar one myself—will also know that there are many aspects of the 'supernatural' that are taken for granted there; for example, there are 'wart charmers' who really *can* make warts disappear in a day or so by muttering a charm. There are dowsers who can not only locate underground water, but who can discover the sex of an unborn child by swinging a pendulum over the mother's stomach. When David Conway was four, he was taken to see a local farmer, a Mr James of Plynlimon, who made up various herbal remedies that he dispensed throughout the district. The odd thing about these remedies is that they worked. Conway was so fascinated by it all, that he learned all that Mr James could teach him about herbal law (and has since written a book about it). At the age of seven, he found an adult reader's ticket to the local library, which had a fairly good 'occult' section—no doubt consisting largely of works like Harry Price's *Most Haunted House in England*; young Conway hurled himself on it, and soon had a wide and comprehensive working knowledge of 'the occult'. But Mr James remained his chief mentor, introducing him to astrology as well as herbalism, and to the simple basic principles of ordinary 'white magic'. Someone should persuade him to write a book about his apprenticeship with the Welsh farmer; from hints he has dropped, I suspect it would be as fascinating as Carlos Castaneda's accounts of Don Juan, as well as being rather more truthful.

Meeting Mr James was the best piece of luck of Conway's early years, for he was able to absorb all the basic principles of 'mysticism' (for that is what it amounts to) at an early age, before the 'shades of the prison house' began to close on the growing youth. For he admits that at university, he did his best to seem like all the other graduates and forgot magic. His few attempts to explore spiritualism, theosophy and contemporary witchcraft soon ended in disillusionment—or boredom. He does not explain why, but I presume it was for the same reason that I felt repelled by my own contacts with spiritualism as a child and teenager. My grandparents were spiritualists; it seemed somehow too vague, too imprecise, too human—*all too human*. But his early magical training provided him with a solid foundation, and in his early thirties, David Conway decided that he would try to do what no one seemed to have attempted—to write about magic from the point of view of an objective observer *and* a believer. The result was the present volume, which seems to me to be wholly successful in achieving its aims.

And do I actually believe in magic? The question embarrasses me because I dislike the word. It is a pity we cannot have done with it, and invent some other word, or phrase, that links the subject with psychical research and paranormal phenomena. Then I would not have the least hesitation in answering in the affirmative.

I believe that man has two 'wills'—one associated with left-brain consciousness, the other with the right. The left will can bring great precision to bear, but it lacks force. The right will, like an elephant, has great force, but it lacks precision. Magical disciplines must be seen as an attempt to somehow teach the 'right will' (which some occultists prefer to call 'the true will') how to discipline its own forces. Like a snake in a basket, this consciousness responds to music (or symbols) rather than to ideas. I would draw the reader's attention particularly to Chapter 4 of Part One, where Mr Conway describes the art of 'visualization'. It underlines the important point that the only certain way of calling upon the forces of the right hemisphere is through the use of controlled imagination.

If anyone wishes to take this as an admission that the whole subject is moonshine, neither I nor Mr Conway will be in the least bothered. This book is plainly not for them. Those of a more enquiring turn of the mind may care to ponder why the word 'moonshine' is so often used as a synonym for imagination. The answer will provide them with a good introductory insight into the world of the paranormal.

# 8

# Afterword: *Glastonbury: Ancient Avalon, New Jerusalem* (D28)

edited by Anthony Roberts
London: Rider, 1978.

A great deal of this book is intended for readers who are already familiar with the notion of ley lines, power centres and terrestrial zodiacs. But there must still be many who have only a nodding acquaintance with such ideas, and who consequently find many of the contributions completely baffling. So let me start by making allowance for these neophytes and explaining briefly the curious occult philosophy of leys that has begun to emerge in the past ten years and which is still in a vigorous state of development.

Shortly after the war, a retired solicitor named Guy Underwood, who had spent most of his life at Bradford-on-Avon (not far from Stonehenge), decided to devote the days of his retirement to studying some of the prehistoric sites that abound in Wiltshire. His approach to the problem would strike many archaeologists as highly eccentric, for his chief instrument of exploration was a dowsing rod.

Nowadays, it is moderately respectable to talk about dowsing, since authorities like Sir William Barrett have written books on the subject. A century ago, it was widely regarded as a rural superstition, like fairies or wishing wells; Sabine Baring-Gould has a chapter on dowsing in a book called *Curious Myths of the Middle Ages*, where it can be found among chapters on Prester John, the Wandering Jew, and the Holy Grail. In fact, the majority of people nowadays would probably agree that dowsers do seem to be able to locate water, and that it is simply another of those unexplained phenomena like flashes of precognition ('I *knew* we'd get a letter from Aunt Jane this morning'), or the fakir's ability to lie on a bed of nails. It is less widely realized that *most* people can dowse—my own estimate is nine out of ten—and that practically all children can do it first time. No one quite knows why a forked twig—or two strips of plastic tied together at the end—will twist downwards when they pass over underground water; but for some reason, they do. Further speculation must wait until later.

Why did Guy Underwood choose to investigate prehistoric sites with a dowsing rod? Because he wanted to test an assertion by two other dowsers, Captain Robert Boothby and Reginald Smith, that most prehistoric sites are constructed over water— either underground streams or blind springs (springs that never reach the surface). A few weeks' investigation convinced him of the correctness of this claim. Above long barrows and hillside figures cut in the chalk, the rod responded negatively, as it always did for water—that is, the left hand took most of the 'pull'. But at this point, he began to detect another force that caused a positive response—a pull on the right hand. It seemed to be some kind of magnetic force, and this came in two distinct varieties, one wide and one narrow. He called the wide variety aqua stats' and the narrow ones 'track lines'. And all three seemed to play an important part in the placing of holy sites like Stonehenge. In fact, aqua stats and water lines often seemed to run together along the same course. When this happened, they seemed to play an important part in laying out sacred sites, and for this reason Underwood called them 'holy lines'.

The baffling question, of course, was *why* ancient man should have wanted to construct his sacred sites on underground springs, or whatever. What difference could it possibly make? But then, this is part of an even larger question. Why did he want to erect so many standing stones anyway? Barrows are understandable, since they are ancient graves or tombs. And a circle like Stonehenge looks a little like a temple—one can easily imagine strange torch-light ceremonies taking place there, and crowds of worshippers kneeling to the rising sun. But the average stone circle—like Boscawen-Un in Cornwall or the Rollright Stones in Oxfordshire, or Long Meg and her daughters near Penrith—doesn't look in the least like an ancient temple. It would seem just as logical to think of them as the site of some prehistoric game—perhaps an early form of baseball or rounders....

In 1921 a Hereford businessman named Alfred Watkins thought he had discovered an important clue. He seems to have been riding around the countryside on 30 June when he observed that various farm gates, stones, churches, and ancient mounds seemed to fall on straight lines. Study of Ordnance Survey maps verified his suspicion; it seemed clear that many sacred sites *do*, for some reason, lie in straight lines. Single upright stones are often used to mark these 'lines' in valleys. Watkins concluded that the lines, which he called 'leys', were intended as trade routes in a land without roads.

If that was so, then the upright stones were little more than milestones. But if Underwood was right, they were rather more than that, for they were placed above areas to which his dowsing rod responded strongly. That made little sense either....

In the late 1960s, a scholarly recluse named John Michell combined both ideas into a new theory—although it is unlikely that he had read Underwood's *Pattern of the Past*, published posthumously in 1969. Michell pointed out that the Chinese also have their own equivalent of ley lines, which they call dragon paths, or *lung mei*; they believe they are the lines of some sacred earth force and built temples at important intersections. Oddly enough, numerous ley lines in England are associated with dragons, for many churches dedicated to St Michael stand on leys, and St Michael (like St George)

71

is a traditional dragon killer. Another enthusiastic student of these matters, the late T. C. Lethbridge, pointed out that many churches dedicated to St Michael are built on ancient pagan sites dedicated to the sun-god Lugh (a Celtic version of Lucifer); St Michael was Lucifer's leading opponent. The Church took over the pagan site for its place of worship and replaced Lucifer with his Christian opposite. But then, *why* did the Church want to build its places of worship on the sites of old pagan temples? You would have thought they'd have avoided such 'unholy' places. Could it, Lethbridge wondered, have been something in the earth itself that made the place holy? This is a strange idea to the modern mind, for which holiness is a purely abstract quality associated with faith (i.e., wishful thinking).

There is another basic objection to John Michell's identification of ley lines with the Chinese dragon paths; in China, it is the wandering path—like Chesterton's rolling English road—that is sacred; the straight line is associated with powers of darkness. Yet Underwood himself had provided a kind of answer to that one. His and other geodetic lines often run in straight lines for short distances. And of course, you could quite easily trace a long line, tens of miles long, that *included* 'geodesics' along a great deal of its length.

When Lethbridge visited a stone circle called The Merry Maidens near Penzance in Cornwall, he found that the nineteen stones of the circle seemed to contain some kind of force; when he held a pendulum (an alternative to a dowsing rod) in one hand, and placed the other on the stone, the hand resting on the stone began to tingle as if a mild electric current was running through it, and the pendulum in the other hand began to revolve like an aeroplane propeller. Noting that many stone circles have legends of dancing associated with them— girls turned into stone for dancing on the Sabbath, etc.—he speculated that perhaps prehistoric worshippers somehow *charged* the stones with a kind of vital electricity by dancing round them. But as to what the stones were actually used for, Lethbridge could only offer the suggestion (which he admits to be little more than fantasy) that they might have been intended as beacons for flying saucers!

Oddly enough, the suggestion is not quite as mad as it looks at first sight. John Michell seems to have become interested in ley lines because there had been so many UFO sightings over them—particularly in the area of Warminster, not far from Stonehenge. There have also been many in the area of Glastonbury, particularly around the Tor. Both Warminster and Glastonbury are the crossing points of several leys. Moreover, investigators of the supernatural have observed that ghost and poltergeist phenomena often seem to happen at nodal points on leys (i.e., crossings).

In 1976 I made a series of programmes for BBC 2 on various occult phenomena, and one was about Ardachie Lodge, on the edge of Loch Ness. In 1952, a Mr and Mrs MacDonald moved into the lodge as housekeepers and their first night was made highly unpleasant by footsteps, knockings, and the sight of a strange old lady crawling around on all fours with a candle in her hand. The phenomena continued for many months and were investigated by the Society for Psychical Research. The previous owner of the house had been an arthritic old lady, who crawled around the place holding a candle at night.... But Mrs MacDonald insisted she had never had any psychic experience before. They finally left, and the house was pulled down. After the programme had been broadcast in early 1977, I received a letter from a Mr Stephen Jenkins, a Croydon schoolmaster, who told me that Ardachie stood on a crossing point of half a dozen ley lines, all of which he specified with references to the Ordnance Survey map.

Mr Jenkins, I discovered, was something of an expert on leys, having been investigating them for more than a quarter of a century. His interesting book, *The Undiscovered Country*, gives many examples of rather odd phenomena that have taken place on ley lines—especially at nodal points. At a nodal point in Cornwall, as a teenager, he saw a shimmering 'phantom army' which vanished as he took a step forward. Revisiting the spot many years later, after he had learned something about leys, he again saw the 'phantom army' at precisely the same spot. He seems to feel that this is some kind of 'tape recording' of an actual historical event that has remained impressed on the area because of the ley force. He records several instances of becoming curiously dizzy at the nodal points of leys and being totally unable to take his bearings. (I have had a similar experience near Boscawen-Un in Cornwall and have related the incident in my book *Mysteries*.) A party of schoolboys he took to one of the nodal points experienced the same dizziness, although he had taken care not to mention his own experience. Mr Jenkins also mentions a number of 'ghosts' that have been seen on ley lines.

This would certainly not have surprised T. C. Lethbridge.* His own experiences of ghosts and poltergeists (described in his book, *Ghost and Ghoul*) led him also to the conclusion that water has some kind of a 'field' (the force to which the dowsing rod responds), and that this field can somehow record strong emotions. These, in turn, can be picked up accidentally by anyone who is sensitive to them, especially dowsers. Lethbridge knew nothing about leys, but he believed that there are other kinds of field in addition to the one associated with water, and that these can also record events and emotions. In some cases, a whole battle might be recorded (which may explain why so many people have heard booming cannons and the clash of arms at the site of the Battle of Edgehill). All the evidence suggests that crossing points of ley lines provide the ideal conditions for such recordings. This may explain, for example, the ghost that haunts one of the chalets in the back garden of Geoffrey Ashe, at the foot of Glastonbury Tor. The house was once owned by the famous occultist Dion Fortune, who probably used the chalet for magical purposes; now the ghost of an old woman is often seen—or felt—in the chalet. (Mr Ashe tells me that his children pay no attention to it— they feel it is basically benevolent.) Similarly, a Mr John Cox of Highbury has told me of all kinds of curious sights and sounds in an old pub he purchased; perhaps the strangest thing about these phenomena is that he often hears events (i.e., workmen making alterations in a room) *before* they happen, as if the ley— on which the pub stands—causes some kind of 'time slip'.

But perhaps one of the most interesting clues to the actual use of ley lines is offered by Mr Francis Hitching, who remarks that the medicine men of the Sioux Indians in South Dakota renew their powers of healing and second sight by rubbing their spines against a megalith called Standing Rock. This is almost certainly the kind of use to which the standing stones were put by our Stone Age ancestors. Places like Glastonbury Stonehenge, and Avebury were holy because the earth forces were unusually concentrated at such points. Our ancestors must have known of various ways of using these forces. The precise details are a matter for speculation. We know that their religion was connected with the fertility of the earth; perhaps at certain times of the year they were able to redirect these forces in such a way as to ensure the fertility of their land, just as a modern farmer in a desert area might canalize his water and direct it to the fields where it is most necessary. *If* they could canalize the forces, then perhaps the standing stones are not intended simply to mark the route of ley lines, but to redirect the energy into straight lines across country. Stephen Jenkins mentions that Air Marshall Sir Victor Goddard told the British Interplanetary Society in 1969 that UFOs could come from "an invisible world that coincides with the space of our own"— another dimension, so to speak, like the place described by

H. G. Wells in *The Plattner Story*. If so, then perhaps the nodal points of leys form some kind of link between the two worlds. Or perhaps they simply provide the necessary energy to bridge the dimensions. Is it possible that the Neolithic priests who built the outer circle of Stonehenge were also able to use this energy to appeal to 'supernatural' beings? In other words, might nodal points of leys be places where prayers might be heard and answered?

Stephen Jenkins has another fascinating remark that brings me to the subject of this piece. Jenkins spent some time in Tibet, studying Buddhism. He speaks of the legendary Kingdom of Shambhala, the Place of Bliss. When Jenkins asked his teachers where Shambhala was located, they replied that it had once been in the Island of Britain, the Celtic Britain of the last centuries before Christ; it was called Gwynfa, the Place of Bliss, and was located at Glastonbury....

This curious piece of information fits in rather well with what we know about the ancient history of Glastonbury. In the Iron Age—from around 600 BC—the area around the Tor was mostly under water. In the third century BC, there were two 'lake villages' at present-day Meare and Godney, around three miles north-west of Glastonbury; they were built by Celts. And at about this time, Glastonbury seems to have acquired the name of Avalon, which in Celtic mythology refers to a rendezvous with the dead. So again, it seems that we have a legend of a place that formed a link between two worlds. (The twelfth-century historian Giraldus Cambrensis declares that Glastonbury is Avalon, and that King Arthur lies buried there.) In his book, *King Arthur's Avalon*, Geoffrey Ashe suggests that the area of the Tor was used by these Celtic settlements as a burial place for their dead—hence the name. But Ashe was writing in 1956, more than a decade before the rediscovery of leys. Nowadays, I suspect, he might be willing to concede that the notion of a *rendezvous* with the dead might well indicate a place that stands 'between two worlds', as well as a burial ground.

In due course, Christianity arrived in Britain. And, as one might expect, Glastonbury soon became a centre of this new religion. That was a logical thing to happen, if Lethbridge is correct. The old 'isle of glass' (Yns-witrin) had been a holy centre perhaps for many centuries before the Celts arrived. Modern carbon-fourteen dating has shown that the outer ditch of Stonehenge—with all its astronomical alignments— was constructed as long ago as the New Stone Age. From this information, Dr Euan MacKie has argued convincingly that the society that built Stonehenge had a highly organized priestly caste, a religious elite. The same people almost certainly constructed the nearby Silbury (which looks like a smaller Glastonbury Tor). It is therefore perfectly conceivable that Glastonbury Tor was another key centre of the ancient fertility religion. The early Christians took it over because they also felt that its power could be used for religious purposes. Significantly, they built a chapel to St Michael (supplanter of the dragon) on top of the Tor.

To ley hunters, it is also significant that the so-called Great Ley runs right through Glastonbury Tor as well as through the Avebury stone circle. The Great Ley is the longest straight line that can be drawn across southern England. It is also—perhaps coincidentally—the line of the midsummer sunrise. It begins at St Michael's Mount in Cornwall, runs across Bodmin Moor and Dartmoor, through many places dedicated to St Michael, and joins the coast of East Anglia near Bury St Edmunds. There are a surprising number of St Michael's churches along this line—at Avebury, Buckland Dinham, the Tor, Othery, Burrow Mount, Lyng, Creech St Michael, Trull, Brent Tor, and St Michael's Mount itself. All these churches also have associations with dragons, which are often portrayed carved into the fabric and in the stained-glass windows.

So what does all this amount to? Basically, the notion that ancient man was far closer to the earth than his modern descendants and had entered into an altogether more symbiotic relationship with it. His religion was based upon the forces of the earth, upon which his existence depended, and he recognized that these forces varied in strength according to the positions of the heavens. This is why he was also an expert in astronomy and why his temples, like Stonehenge and Callanish (in the Hebrides), were also vast stone computers for predicting eclipses of the sun and moon. He may have known how to use these earth forces in many ways: to bring fertility to the land, to increase his own psychic powers (modern primitive tribes still rely on their shaman or priest to tell them where they can expect to find herds of deer or other animals), perhaps even to perform acts of magic. (Lethbridge suggested, half seriously, that the forces could have been used in erecting the great sarsens of Stonehenge. I myself have noted that Uri Geller often places his foot against some 'earthed' object, like a radiator, in order to gain the power to bend metal or stop watches, and have wondered whether he may not be somehow making use of the earth force.)

All this sounds reasonable enough. But the most surprising part is still to come. John Michell pointed out that many of the landmarks on ley lines seem designed to be seen *from the air*. (The famous snake mound in Ohio is an example.) That curious enthusiast Erich von Däniken has also pointed out many prehistoric sites — like the Nazca lines in Peru — seem to be designed to be visible from above. Lethbridge, as we have seen, speculated (half-jokingly) that the stone circles were intended to 'guide in' ancient spacecraft. If, in fact, we can stretch our imagination to the point of believing that the earth might have been visited by spacemen in prehistoric times, then there is nothing wildly improbable about this theory. The stone circles may not have been *built* to guide in flying saucers, but if the spacecraft had instruments that could measure the earth's magnetic field, then they may well have used the stone circles as beacons at night.

Now back in the age of the first Queen Elizabeth, her astrologer Dr John Dee visited Glastonbury, drew a map of some of its principal features, and came to the conclusion that many constellations of the heavens were deliberately reflected in man-made earthworks. He called this 'Merlin's secret', and apparently felt that one of the basic shapes of this pattern was that of a horse. (This would have interested Lethbridge, who felt that many ancient sites are connected with the Celtic horse goddess Epona.)

In the 1920s, another student of Glastonbury, Mrs Katharine Maltwood, studied maps of the area and reached the astonishing conclusion that someone had taken the trouble to draw a vast zodiac on the countryside around the Tor. She knew about the effigy mounds in America in the shapes of animals, birds and reptiles. She knew that the legends of the Holy Grail have often been connected with Avalon, but rejected the notion that the Arthurian Grail is the *only* one. She spoke of "an earlier Grail, that 'Cauldron of Wisdom' already famous ages before Joseph of Arimathea brought his message here". In short, Mrs Maltwood concluded that men in remote ages of the past had deliberately used certain natural features of the landscape to sketch vast drawings of the signs of the zodiac on the Glastonbury landscape. She seems to have had no clear idea of why anyone should do this, and certainly no suspicion that the whole thing was designed to be seen from the air. When her book about Glastonbury, 'Temple of the Stars' appeared in 1929, it convinced few people; most readers probably thought it an amusing but totally wild theory. In recent years, discoveries about leys have suddenly made it seem altogether less preposterous. As the reader will have discovered, the majority of contributors to this book accept

Mrs Maltwood's ideas; some have even added their own interesting elaborations and refinements.

I have to confess that I am by no means wholly convinced. As far as I am concerned, one piece of vital evidence is missing. Dr Michael Dames has argued persuasively that Silbury Hill was built to represent a woman crouching in the position of childbirth, and that at the harvest festival the moon was reflected in a lake between her thighs to give the impression that the baby's head was emerging. He also suggests that this could be seen by the whole tribe, which stood on the hill. The whole ley theory seems to demand that the temples could actually be used for religious purposes. And I find it very hard to imagine how Glastonbury's 'Temple of the Stars' could have been used in any practical way. I am willing, I should add, to be convinced. But for me, the mere demonstration that various configurations of the land *could* be the signs of the zodiac is no convincing proof. I would need to be told precisely how the worshippers used the Zodiac in their religious ceremonies.

I am aware that sceptics will dismiss this whole theory about Glastonbury as a tissue of moonshine. They will argue that Glastonbury Tor is a striking landmark that looks as if it came straight out of a fairy tale, and that this has simply stimulated the imagination of various writers with a romantic bent. John Cowper Powys set his *Glastonbury Romance* there for no other reason, as far as I can see. But anyone who takes the trouble to start at the beginning—with the works of Professor Thom on the astronomical alignments of the megalithic monuments, and the speculations of historians on their purpose—will probably end by being convinced that there is some strange mystery here, almost certainly connected with an ancient fertility religion which may date from many thousands of years before Christ. Even Margaret Murray's astonishing speculations about the 'old religion' of the witches begin to look like inspired guesses. We may reserve the right to doubt whether

Glastonbury is really the ancient Shambhala, or even whether its Zodiac was constructed deliberately. But eventually, there can surely be little doubt that this was once one of the holy centres of England—perhaps of Europe—and that some of the most important and exciting discoveries about its purpose are still to come.

**Notes:**

* See also Chapter 4. *Ed.*

9

# Foreword: *The Rosy Cross Unveiled: the History, Mythology and Rituals of an Occult Order* (D35)

by Christopher McIntosh
Wellingborough, Northants: Aquarian Press, 1980.

In 1895, W. B. Yeats wrote an essay titled "The Body of the Father Christian Rosencrux," which begins by describing how the founder of Rosicrucianism was laid in a noble tomb, surrounded by inextinguishable lamps, where he lay for many generations, until he was discovered by chance by students of the same magical order. Having said this, Yeats goes on to attack modern criticism for entombing the imagination, proclaiming that "the ancients and the Elizabethans abandoned themselves to imagination as a woman abandons herself to love, and created beings who made the people of this world seem but shadows...."

On the whole, Yeats' use of the image of Christian Rosenkreuz seems irrelevant until the reader comes to this sentence: "I cannot get it out of my mind that this age of criticism is about to pass, and an age of imagination, of emotion, of moods, of revelation, about to come in its place; for certainly belief in a supersensual world is at hand...." In this statement, Yeats shows his own deep understanding of the whole Rosicrucian phenomenon. *That* is what it was really about; that is the real explanation to reverberate down three-and-a-half centuries.

The "hoax" began—as Christopher McIntosh describes in these pages—with the publication, in 1614, of a pamphlet called *Fama Fraternitatis of the Meritorious Order of the Rosy Cross*, which purported to describe the life of the mystic-magician Christian

Rosenkreuz, who lived to be 106, and whose body was carefully concealed in a mysterious tomb for the next 120 years. The author of the present book translates "fama" as "declaration," but my own Latin dictionary defines it as "common talk...a report, rumour, saying, tradition." So it would hardly be unfair to translate "fama" as myth or legend.

At all events, this mysterious pamphlet (which can be found printed in full as an appendix to *The Rosicrucian Enlightenment* by Frances Yates*) goes on to invite all interested parties to join the Brotherhood and tells them that they have only to make their interest known — either by word of mouth or in writing — and the Brotherhood will hear about it, and probably make contact. This is, in itself, a suggestion that the Brotherhood has magical powers — perhaps some crystal ball that will enable them to "tune in" to anyone who is genuinely interested.

Two more works followed the pamphlet — as Mr. McIntosh relates — and many people took the trouble to publish replies, indicating their eagerness to join the Brotherhood. No one, as far as anyone knows, ever heard from the Brotherhood. Yet the very idea of their existence caused tremendous excitement. This is what everybody had been waiting for — a kind of prophecy of a Second Coming: "Howbeit we know that after a time there will now be a general reformation, both of divine and human things, according to our desire...." 'The land of heart's desire' was about to become a reality.

Christopher McIntosh suggests, very plausibly I think, that the first two pamphlets were probably a joint effort of a group of idealistic philosophers based in Tübingen, perhaps inspired by an early 'novel' by one of their number, Johann Valentin Andreae. This 'novel,' *The Chemical Wedding of Christian Rosencreutz*, was published as the third 'Rosicrucian' document in 1616.

All of this raises interesting questions: Why did the Brotherhood ask for volunteers and recruits if they had no intention of replying? If the authors of these documents were idealistic, then what was the ultimate aim of the whole exercise?

The main clue to the answer, I believe, lies in a phrase in Johann Andreae's will, made in 1634, when he was 48. Andreae writes: "Though I now leave the Fraternity itself, I shall never leave the true Christian Fraternity, which beneath the Cross, smells of the rose, and is quite apart from the filth of this century." 'The filth of this century'; 'this filthy century' — either phrase might have been used by W. B. Yeats if his language had been a little more emphatic.

In his autobiography, Yeats says that Ruskin once remarked to his father that, as he made his daily way to the British Museum, he saw the faces around him becoming more and more corrupt. Untrue of course: people don't really change that much — or that fast. But Ruskin's words express the hunger of a man who feels that he lives in an age when no one really cares about the things that matter. T. S. Eliot expressed the same feeling in *The Waste Land* and *The Hollow Men*. The invention of Christian Rosenkreuz is, likewise, not so much a hoax as a cry of rejection and a demand for new ways: in short, a kind of prophecy.

It is worth noting that there are apparently two kinds of legend that seem to exercise great fascination over the minds of men. The first involves wickedness or horror — Faust, Frankenstein, Dracula, Sweeney Todd, even Jack the Ripper. The second involves, not so much goodness as greatness, superhumanity; and this can be found in legends of Hermes Trismegistos, King Arthur, Parsifal, and Merlin, as well as the modern *Superman* and *Batman* comic strips. In "Hellas," Shelley used the figure of an old Jew to portray this type — the Wandering Jew of the Bible — who lives "in a sea cavern amid the Demonesi," and who is a master of all wisdom. Yeats later remarked that he joined the Theosophical Society because he wanted to believe in the real existence of the Old Jew "or his like."

For, of course, both the "magical" organizations to which Yeats belonged—the Theosophical Society and the Golden Dawn—drew a leaf out of Pastor Andreae's book and set out to build their organizations on a myth propagated as reality. Madame Blavatsky claimed to be in communication with Secret Masters in Tibet. And the story behind the Golden Dawn was at least as circumstantial as the account of the life of Rosenkreuz. In 1885, according to this story, a clergyman named Woodford was rummaging through the books in a second-hand stall in Farringdon Road when he came across a manuscript written in cipher; a friend, Dr William Wynn Westcott, identified the cipher as one invented by a 15th-century alchemist, Trithemius. It proved to contain five magical rituals for introducing newcomers into a secret society. In the manuscript, there was also a letter which stated that anyone interested in the rituals should contact a certain Fräulein Sprengel in Stuttgart. It was Fräulein Sprengel, the representative of a German magical order, who gave Westcott permission to found the Golden Dawn.

The cipher manuscript may just possibly have existed (although it was not picked up in a bookstall in Farringdon Road). The letter about Fräulein Sprengel certainly did not, nor did that lady herself. Yet the story accomplished its effect, and the Golden Dawn grew into one of the most impressive magical organizations of the late 19th century. And—as Mr McIntosh relates—the legend of Christian Rosenkreuz came to play a central part in its magical procedures.

A few decades ago, the Golden Dawn was held in very low esteem by literary scholars who had heard about it. I remember attending evening classes on Yeats soon after the War, and our teacher, Professor Philip Collins, remarking that he had expected to find Yeats' comments about magic and occultism completely preposterous, and was surprised to find that they had a reassuring ring of common sense. All the same, he took it entirely for granted that the Golden Dawn was a society created by charlatans and supported by the gullible. I daresay most professors of modern literature still take that view.

But there are now a great many students of the 'paranormal', who are willing to acknowledge that, in some strange way, 'magic' can produce extraordinary effects. Anyone who doubts this should read Yeats' essay on magic where he describes in detail a magical operation conducted by MacGregor Mathers (another founder of the Golden Dawn) and his wife, in which Mathers was able to take control of Yeats' imagination and induce curious visions.

It is important to recognize that "magic" usually involves the control of mental states rather than the production of physical effects upon matter—witches flying on broomsticks, etc.—although physical effects *can* be produced. The mental effects all take their starting point from telepathy, while the physical ones may be regarded as deliberately induced 'poltergeist effects', in which objects are made to move by some curious power of the unconscious mind. (I have come increasingly to believe that the right half of the brain is involved here, and that the actual energy used is the same energy that causes a dowsing rod to twist in the hands of the water diviner—probably some form of Earth magnetism that can be channelled by the right cerebral hemisphere). It seems perfectly clear that Mathers had learned the trick of controlling these generally unrecognized energies.

I agree that there appears, at first sight, to be little connection between this concept of 'magic' and the history of Rosicrucianism, as explained in the following pages by Christopher McIntosh. Yet in the course of reading his book, I have come to feel the connection increasingly strongly. It began to crystallize when I read his account of Heraclitus of Ephesus (in chapter 1), who believed that the universe dies like a living organism and leaves behind a seed from which a new universe originates. Everything in the cosmos derives from a basic substance, a kind of fire, and everything moves in a cyclical process.

Just before reading this, I had been writing an outline of a book on astronomy and had been describing the Big Bang Theory of the universe. Heraclitus described this with some precision. According to the Big Bang Theory—for which the evidence is now overwhelming—the universe *did* begin (around ten billion years ago) as pure, undifferentiated "fire", from which the elements were to crystallize later. It will continue to expand for another few billion years, until its own gravity causes it to collapse again. It will eventually become a concentrated mass of matter, whose size will be far larger than the "critical mass" needed to create a Black Hole. But then, according to the latest astronomical theory, a Black Hole does not go on collapsing into itself indefinitely, but eventually explodes once more. If this is correct, then Heraclitus's scheme would be weirdly accurate. In fact, the only thing Heraclitus failed to grasp was that the new "seed" would be smaller than the previous one because so much energy would have been irrecoverably lost in the whole process.

Now you may say that Heraclitus was only making an 'informed guess' about the universe. But when a guess comes this close to reality, I personally begin to wonder whether it could not be something more than guesswork. That is, whether there is not some other way of knowing the universe, directly and intuitively. Mystics have always said so, and in his remarkable *Drug Taker's Notes*, R. H. Ward speaks of a 'mystical' experience he had under dental anaesthetic. He says that after the first few inhalations, he passed "directly into a state of consciousness already far more complete than the fullest degree of ordinary waking consciousness." He repeats this point several times, speaking of how "consciousness diminished" again toward ordinary consciousness, and how "the darkness of what we flatter ourselves is consciousness closed in upon me" (i.e., as he was once more waking up). Even more interesting, however, is Ward's description of passing through what he calls "a region of ideas", where the insight was intellectual rather than emotional. He adds: "One knew not merely one thing here and another thing there...one knew everything there is to know."** Robert Graves has described a similar mystical experience in a story called *The Abominable Mr. Gunn* (he told me it was autobiographical), and here again it is clear that the sense of 'knowing everything' is meant in a literal sense, as if we had some strange faculty that could reach out and acquire *any* piece of knowledge at will.

*If* there is anything in this theory, it may be that there *is* a tradition of knowledge that precedes the development of modern intellectual consciousness. This could explain why Neolithic man went to the trouble of building vast stone computers like Stonehenge more than two millennia before the Chaldeans, who are usually given the credit for being the first astronomers, began to study the heavens.

At all events, it seems clear that the doctrines of Christian Rosenkreuz were based on those of the Gnostics, and on the notion which Christopher McIntosh has expressed so admirably by the analogy of man being 'under water', with the region of knowledge and insight above the surface. T. S. Eliot said much the same thing in a chorus from his poem, "The Rock".

Fundamentally, then, I am not speaking about a hoax, or even about 'wishful thinking', but about the most profound problem of the human race. Again, Ward comes excitingly close to putting his finger on it when he says that a part of him disliked his mother for "making him live two lives" — the natural instinctive life of a child, and the superimposed and artificial life of 'the world'. He goes on to say that, under LSD, it seemed to him that all children are ruined by adults through being conditioned to the life of this world so that they live two lives, one secretly, and one for adult approval. But then 'ruin' is not inevitable.

For example, all my own books, from *The Outsider* onward, have been about precisely this subject: the 'outsider's' rejection of 'the world', his desire to turn inward to a world of truth that he feels resides in his own depths. So, plainly, I have not been entirely ruined. Ward himself remarks that he is surprised that he is not more wicked and madder than he is, considering his upbringing. Most of us do, in fact, survive, because that inner hunger is so intense.

*This*, I believe, explains why Rosicrucianism has continued to exert its grip on the Western mind. It is not because we are hopelessly gullible, or because we would like to believe in absurd fantasies. In a legend like that of Christian Rosenkreuz, we seem to catch a glimpse of what we *ought* to be, and what we *could* be. If we set about it with sufficient determination, the grip of 'the world' can be broken—or at least weakened until it ceases to induce a constant feeling of alienation. We are a planet of a double star, torn between two powerful gravitational forces. We have to learn to move inward without losing control over the external world and not, like Rimbaud, simply surrendering ourselves to an "ordered derangement of the senses".

I am not, of course, denying that much of the current interest in occultism has its root in 'escapism' of the most ordinary kind; but I still believe that it is the *real* content of 'occultism' that attracts powerful minds. Christopher McIntosh strikes me as an interesting illustration of this proposition. It is only necessary to glance at this book to see that his is a trained mind working within the academic tradition. His first book, *The Astrologers and their Creed* (1969), is basically a brilliant piece of research into the history of astrology. In the very last chapter, "The Verdict on Astrology", McIntosh concedes that it cannot be defended scientifically; but he goes on to cite the researches of the Gauquelins into the actual statistics about people born under Mars, Saturn, Jupiter, etc., to show that there *does* now appear to be some solid scientific basis for believing that human temperament is influenced by the planets. You could say that the book is sceptical until the last two pages.

McIntosh's next work, *Eliphas Lévi and the French Occult*

*Revival* is again, quite simply, an excellent piece of biographical research—one of the few books on this important 'magician' in English. At no point does he seem to give too much credit to Lévi's magical claims. He is interested in Lévi as a personality and as a thinker, but not really as a mage.

Before writing this foreword, I asked McIntosh to tell me how he became interested in the Rosicrucians. His reply was immensely interesting. He related that he had been interested in 'occult' subjects since he was an undergraduate at Oxford in the early 1960s. He came across many references to the Rosicrucians, but A. E. Waite's enormous and turgid volume left him confused. Since he had always enjoyed writing things that gave him the opportunity of doing some detective work—especially when it involved reading in French and German—he settled down to studying the original sources. The book was started in 1972, the year *Lévi* came out.

During the course of writing the book, however, McIntosh's attitude toward his subject changed:

"When I began it, I was going through a phase of rather dry, scholarly objectivity in my attitude to such subjects and I intended to examine Rosicrucianism simply as a rather curious historical phenomenon without really expecting to find that it contained a teaching of any real depth or coherence. Since then, not only has my attitude changed—I have become much more pro-occult—but I also found during my researches that Rosicrucianism goes deeper than I had realized, and does contain something valuable and coherent. So you could say that this book has been an important experience in my life. It has taught me that, sooner or later, anyone studying these subjects from an academic point of view has to make the decision whether they are going to take a personal stance for or against. To turn away from this decision and try to remain neutral is, to me, death."

McIntosh goes on to apologize for not having conveyed this sense of the real inner meaning of Rosicrucianism sufficiently. But having read his manuscript for the second time, I can reassure him. I have also read most of the major texts on the subject, so I am in a position to assure him that his own is far and away the best. And since it also happens to be an interesting and exciting story, it should at last secure for the mysterious Rosenkreuz the interest he deserves.

**Notes:**
* *The Rosicrucian Enlightenment* London: Routledge & Kegan Paul, 1972), p. 238.
** R. H. Ward, *Drug Taker's Notes* (London: Victor Gollancz 1957), pp. 26-28

# 10

# Introduction: *Healing Energy, Prayer and Relaxation* (D45)

by Dr Israel Regardie
Las Vegas: Golden Dawn Publications, 1982.

The author of this small and fascinating book is the last living representative of the great 'occult tradition' of the late 19th century, whose major names include Madame Blavatsky, W. B. Yeats, MacGregor Mathers, A. E. Waite, Aleister Crowley and Dion Fortune. Even in such distinguished company, Regardie stands out as a figure of central importance.

Francis Israel Regardie was born in London on November 17, 1907 and moved with his family to America in 1921. He attended art school in Philadelphia until, in his own words, "I realized I was no artist." Fate had marked him out for a rather more strange and interesting career. He received its first intimations when he was fifteen years old and saw a reference to Madame Blavatsky in a book belonging to his sister. Intrigued by the name, he looked it up, and learned about the eventful career of that tempestuous lady. "From then on", he says, "I was hooked." The interest in Madame Blavatsky extended to Hindu philosophy and to the practice of yoga, and by the time he was eighteen, Regardie was familiar with the major works on yoga.

So it was with considerable excitement that, at the house of an attorney friend in Washington D.C., he made the discovery of a new text on yoga by a man who unmistakably knew what he was talking about. The work—which was read aloud—was called, rather cryptically, *Part I of Book IV*, and was by one Aleister Crowley. Regardie was so excited that he wrote to Crowley at the address of the publisher. And he had totally forgotten about it when, some eight months later, he received a reply from Paris. Crowley suggested that Regardie should get in touch with his New York agent, a German named Karl Germer. Regardie went to New York to meet Germer and found that this ex-Wehrmacht officer regarded Crowley with enormous admiration. He sold Regardie a set of a work called *The Equinox*, a magazine that Crowley had published between 1909 and 1914. And for the next few months, Regardie plunged into an altogether strange world of magic, mysticism, occult philosophy and Nietzschean aphorism, all tinged with a distinct flavour of the 1890s. The result was that two years later, in October 1928, Regardie sailed for France, and was met at the Gare St. Lazare by Crowley; 'the Great Beast' had invited Regardie to become his secretary.

The next two or three years must have been a traumatic experience for the young Americanized Londoner. Crowley had just published his most important book, *Magick in Theory and Practice*, which had failed to attract much attention; a quarrel with the book's press agent led to the agent telling the police that Crowley was a drug addict. As a result, Crowley was expelled from Paris, and his new secretary, who had failed to obtain a residence permit, was also ordered to leave. Because of his association with Crowley, he was not allowed to land in England—although he had a British passport—and had to go to Brussels. It took him six more months before he was allowed to land in England. There he moved in with Crowley and his wife at a house at Knockholt, in Kent, and began preparing some of Crowley's works for the press—Crowley had discovered a publisher called P. R. Stephensen, who ran Mandrake Press. Unfortunately, Crowley's reputation as the 'wickedest man in the world' was now so firmly established that his books aroused widespread opposition among booksellers, and the press soon went bankrupt. Meanwhile, Regardie and Stephensen collaborated on a short book in defence of Crowley, *The Legend of Aleister Crowley*. It did nothing to improve Crowley's sinister reputation, or to improve the finances of Mandrake Press. And so, Crowley went his own way, and Regardie went his. He became the secretary to the writer Thomas Burke, author of the once-famous *Limehouse Nights*, and he also wrote his own first two books, *The Garden of the Pomegranates* and *The Tree of Life*. Both are studies in the Hebrew magical system, the Qabalah, and the latter is regarded by many as one of the most important books on 'magic' ever written. It is dedicated "with poignant memory of what might have been, to Marsyas." The latter is Crowley. And it is sad to record that when Regardie sent copies of one of his books to Crowley, the latter received it with something less than appreciation, and made some unkind jokes, particularly about Regardie's adoption of the name Francis—a name that had been bestowed on him by a woman friend who, like Regardie, was an admirer of St. Francis. Regardie gave way to outraged vanity, and wrote Crowley a sarcastic letter, addressing him as 'Alice', a possible reference to the 'Beast's' homosexual inclinations as well as a diminutive of his name. The result was a complete break between the two; Crowley produced a scurrilous document about his ex-secretary, accusing him of theft and betrayal, which he circulated to all Regardie's friends and acquaintances. It says a great deal for Regardie's forgiving nature—and for his capacity for objective admiration—that he has reproduced this document in full in his later study of Crowley, *The Eye in the Triangle*.

After the publication of *The Tree of Life*, Regardie found himself at the centre of a violent controversy. He had discussed some of the magical practices of the society known as the Golden Dawn, of which Crowley had been a highly disruptive member in the early years of the century. Some ex-members attacked him; others—like Dion Fortune—supported him. The upshot was that he was invited to join the Stella Matutina, a magical order based upon the original Golden Dawn. This he found an immense disappointment. As 'magicians' the chiefs of the Stella

Matutina struck him as ignorant and inept. In disgust, he left the order, and decided to publish the rituals of the Golden Dawn — an act that has earned him much odium in 'occult' circles, although every student of the history of occultism remains in his debt.

These details are necessary so that readers of this book should understand something of Regardie's importance in the history of 20th century 'occultism'. The remainder may be told more briefly. Regardie remained in England until 1937, continuing to study magic and alchemy, and writing another important text, *The Philosopher's Stone*, about the mysteries of alchemy. This is one of the most interesting and exciting things he ever wrote; it is basically a Jungian interpretation of alchemy as a search for some kind of unity of being, an attempt to unite conscious and unconscious forces of the psyche. (It is all the more fascinating in that in more recent years, Regardie changed his mind to some extent, and came to believe that alchemy is an attempt at a chemical transformation of matter—I tell the whole story in my book *Mysteries*.) And, in 1937, recognizing that war was inevitable, Regardie returned to the United States. Here he threw himself into the study of psychology—he had undergone Freudian analysis in England—and became a lay analyst. When America entered the war, he enlisted in the army—a step he wryly admits to have been "a ghastly error" After the war, he obtained his doctorate in psychology, moved to California, and practiced Reichian therapy. He admits that this, "with Magick, has changed the course of my whole life." In 1980, he retired to Arizona, where he continues to write.*

For many years now, I have been an avid reader of Regardie's books. The last one I read, *Foundations of Practical Magic*, was published in England in 1979. It fascinated me because it reveals that, with age, Regardie's mind becomes more clear and vigorous—a tribute to the disciplines to which he has devoted his life. But the chapter that impressed me most was not concerned with magic, but with meditation. It is a remarkable synthesis of all he knows about magic, meditation and psychotherapy.

Now for those who—understandably—regard magic as an absurd superstition, it is important to bear in mind Crowley's own definitions: "Magick is the Science and Art of causing Change to occur in conformity with the Will." He is echoing a remark of the great 19th century occultist Eliphas Levi, who wrote: "Would you learn to reign over yourself and others? Learn how to will." Many students of magic are, no doubt, attracted by its romantic aura, and enjoy indulging in a kind of wishful thinking. But I suspect that the true students of magic have all started from the same intuition: that in some absurd, paradoxical way, *human beings are far stronger than they realize.* Everyone knows that odd feeling we get at times that all is well, that nothing can go wrong. Just as there are days when nothing seems to go right, so there are days when we experience a feeling that is like the first smell of spring: an excitement that seems based on some knowledge, some recognition. The romantic poets of the 19th century were always experiencing these 'moments of vision', and then wondering the next day whether it was all an illusion. Magic' is first of all an attempt to achieve some kind of control over that inner world of intuition. It escapes us because we are so poor at focusing the attention. So one of the first steps in magical practice is to attempt to train the mind to *visualize*, to be capable of 'conjuring up' (and it is interesting that we use this particular phrase about imagining) objects and scenes and giving them 'the smell of reality'. And this ability is, in fact, one of the basic psychological disciplines: that is to say that a person who had become accustomed to doing it at will would have achieved a far higher level of mental health than the rest of us. Students of ritual magic also believe that when a person has achieved this level of intensity, it is, to some extent, possible to 'make things happen' The magician does not, like the wizard in *The Sorceror's Apprentice*, turn brooms into watercarriers; but he believes that it is possible to shape his own destiny. Again, everyone knows the feeling of being completely determined to do something, and how, when this happens, events often seem to 'come out right' Jung would probably say that this is the operation of the immense unknown forces of the unconscious mind.

Regardie believes, as I do, that this knowledge is very old indeed—that it was probably already old when the Egyptians built their first temples. One of the most exciting things in the world is to discover that the latest findings in psychology, in structural linguistics, in split-brain physiology, blend smoothly into the pattern of the earliest recorded human knowledge. It is this insight that pervades this book on healing energy, prayer and relaxation and which makes it, to me, the most personal and moving of all Regardie's writings.


**Notes:**
* Regardie died in 1985. *Ed.*

# 11

# Introduction: *The Night-Side of Nature or, Ghosts and Ghost-Seers*

by Catherine Crowe (D59)

Wellingborough, Northants: Aquarian Press, 1986

Whenever I look at those pages of advertisements at the back of old Victorian novels, I experience a certain melancholy. It is sad to realize how many of the great and famous of the nineteenth century are now totally forgotten. The once-celebrated Bertha H. Buxton can be found next to Honoré de Balzac, while Mrs Gore, Theodore Hook, and Amelia B. Edwards seem to be as highly regarded as Sir Walter Scott, Alexandre Dumas, and Victor Hugo. And, to judge from the advertisements in the back of Routledge's Railway Library, Mrs Catherine Crowe, the author of the present volume, was once as famous as Dickens and Thackeray. Alas, she was incarcerated in a mental home at the height of her career, and thereafter more-or-less forgotten. Yet her book *The Night-Side of Nature* survived her death (in 1876) by at least half a century, and even today remains one of the most readable of the great classics of psychical research.

Biographical details about Mrs Crowe are scarce—this being one of the sad consequences of being predeceased by one's reputation. The *Dictionary of National Biography* states that she was born at Borough Green in Kent in about 1800 and that her maiden name was Stevens. But it says nothing about where she was educated, whom she married, and why she then moved to Edinburgh (although we may presume that it was because her husband was a Scot). To judge by her novels, she was a highly intelligent and imaginative woman, with a good ear for dialogue and a certain flair for languages. We know that she became a 'disciple' of the well-known phrenologist George Combe (phrenology being the belief that human character can be 'read' from the bumps on the skull) and was much influenced by his scepticism about religion and the supernatural. But as she approached her forties, she seems to have become rather more broad-minded, and was fascinated by an extraordinary work called *Die Seherin von Prevorst* (*The Seeress of Prevorst*), which had caused a sensation in Germany when it appeared in 1829. It was a first-hand and highly circumstantial account of a woman with 'supernatural powers', and it converted many sceptical Victorians into taking a more open-minded attitude towards 'the occult'.

In her late thirties, Catherine Crowe produced her first novel *Susan Hopley*, and when this appeared (under the imprint of a London publisher, Saunders and Otley) in 1841, it made her an instant celebrity. (The *Dictionary of National Biography* states that her first novel was *Manorial Rights*, published in 1839, but the London Library's first edition of *Men and Women, or Manorial Rights* is dated 1844, and the author is given as 'the author of "The Adventures of Susan Hopley"'.) I have read it recently and can see exactly why it was so popular. It purports to be the life story of a servant called Susan Hopley, and within a dozen pages the reader finds himself involved in the kind of skulduggery that kept the Victorians reading feverishly until the candle gave out. The villain manages to get himself made part-heir to the fortune of a rich wine merchant, then has him murdered and 'frames' Susan Hopley's brother. Having got the reader thoroughly involved, Mrs Crowe goes off into other plots and sub-plots, which she keeps boiling merrily until they reach their conclusion a thousand pages (and three volumes) later. But her interest in 'the occult' may be gauged from an episode in Chapter Four, when Susan sits dozing by the bedroom fire, awaiting the arrival of her master (the wine merchant), and has a terrifying dream in which she sees her brother 'with dead eyes', then sees her master sitting in a chair with his throat cut. (The actual murder of her brother and his master is taking place at roughly the same time). The next day she hears the news of the murder of her master, and her brother's mysterious disappearance.

*The Adventures of Susan Hopley* or *Circumstantial Evidence* made Mrs Crowe famous—or at least, it would have done if anyone had known she had written it. But the novel appeared without any author's name on the title page—a not unusual proceeding for the period. (If a novel was a failure, then it made no difference, and if it was a success, then the curiosity about the identity of the author would spread its fame). She must have had rather an enjoyable time in the period immediately following its publication, when the news of her authorship of the current bestseller spread by word of mouth. In 1844 came *Men and Women*, which displays the same ability to make the reader want to turn the page. And by now she was sufficiently celebrated to be suspected of the authorship of another anonymous bestseller of 1844, *Vestiges of Creation*, a remarkable work on the subject of evolution which anticipated Darwin by fifteen years. Its author was, in fact, an Edinburgh publisher and historian called Robert Chambers; he was undoubtedly wise to publish anonymously, for his work was condemned as 'Godless' and raised a storm of indignation. That Mrs Crowe was suspected of its authorship— and coyly refused to deny it—seems to indicate that she was regarded by her fellow townspeople as an intelligent and original woman.

In 1845 came her translation (and abridgement) of *The Seeress of Prevorst* by Justinus Kerner. Kerner was a rich and eccentric doctor and a well-known poet, a friend of Goethe who had been practising in Weinsberg in 1826 when he was consulted by relatives of a peasant woman called Friederike Hauffe, who was dying of a wasting disease. Friederike had never been a healthy woman and ever since childhood had been prone to fall into trances and 'see spirits'. That she possessed some paranormal powers was obvious, for she was able to read a book that was placed open on her stomach. Kerner tested her rigorously, but he doubted her ability to see ghosts until she offered him convincing proof. She told Kerner she was being haunted by a man with a squint, and Kerner recognized him from her description as a respectable citizen who had died a few years earlier. His spirit was unable to rest, said Friederike, because he had embezzled some money, and another man had been blamed. He now wanted to make restitution and told Friederike that the proof of his embezzlement would be found in a certain file in the town archives. The document turned up where Friederike had said it would, and Kerner was convinced that her paranormal powers were genuine. For the next three years, he observed her closely and in 1829, the year of her death, created a sensation with *The Seeress of Prevorst*, one of the first — and still one of the greatest — classics of the paranormal.

Catherine Crowe's translation was an instant success, and it finally convinced Mrs Crowe that her mentor George Combe was mistaken in his scepticism about the 'supernatural'. At this point in the nineteenth century there was a powerful reaction against the domination of the Christian Church — the Church that had burned Giordano Bruno, forced Galileo to recant his statement that the earth travelled around the sun, and opposed any form of science that seemed likely to make churchgoers question the most literal interpretation of the Bible. By 1840 it had at last become possible to question the authority of the Bible without risking imprisonment, and because scientists had fought hard for this freedom, they were not willing to admit religion in by the back door in the form of a belief in 'spirits' or life after death. They can hardly be blamed. But when Mrs Crowe came to study the evidence for such matters as apparitions, precognitions of the future, poltergeists, veridical dreams, and telepathy it became clear to her that the sceptics were throwing out the baby with the bath water. A great many tales of the 'supernatural' might be pure superstitious nonsense but many more—like Kerner's account of Friederike—had all the hallmarks of authenticity. She saw that science had simply gone too far in dismissing the supernatural, and her introduction to *The Night-Side of Nature* suggests that when she attempted to express these views to sceptical friends (no doubt George Combe was among them) she met with a 'pharisaical scepticism which denies without investigation'.

But by this time Mrs Crowe was a lady of considerable celebrity, and she was not to be silenced by ridicule; it only put her on her mettle. She was deeply convinced that the correct attitude towards the unknown was an open-minded willingness to investigate.

"And by investigation I do not mean the hasty, captious, angry notice of an unwelcome fact that too frequently claims the right of pronouncing on a question, but the slow, modest, painstaking examination that is content to wait upon nature and humbly follow her disclosures, however opposed to preconceived theories, or mortifying to human pride."

These words were written more than a decade before T. H. Huxley made his famous pronouncement on the duty of a scientist: to "...sit down before fact as a little child, be prepared to give up every preconceived notion, follow humbly wherever and to whatever abysses nature leads, or you shall learn nothing."

The anonymous author of the article in the *Dictionary of National Biography* acknowledges that *The Night-Side of Nature* is "...one of the best collections of supernatural stories in our language", then adds: "It has little value from any other point of view, being exceedingly credulous and uncritical." This is an example of the kind of blind prejudice that no doubt drove Mrs

Crowe to distraction. For what distinguishes her book is, first of all, a certain hard-headed common sense, a characteristic which can also be found in her novels, and a remarkable determination to treat the phenomena in a thoroughly scientific spirit. She is not credulous or uncritical; on the contrary, *The Night-Side of Nature* is the first sustained attempt to treat paranormal phenomena in the scientific spirit that would later characterize the Society for Psychical Research. In that respect, her presentation of the case of the haunted mill house at Willington on Tyne in the chapter on haunted houses, is a classic.

Whatever the attitude of the sceptics, Catherine Crowe's book had the success it deserved. From its first appearance in 1848, it was never out of print for more than a century. What appealed to the Victorians was that Mrs Crowe was obviously not a 'spiritualist' or a hysterical woman in the grip of a semi-religious credulity; she spoke in the calm, rational tones that appealed to them, and her religion was a religion of common sense and decency. Her attitude is summarized in a paragraph in the third volume of her novel *Lily Dawson* (which appeared the year before *The Night-Side of Nature* and was almost as great a success as *Susan Hopley*):

"People who do not live in a continual state of wonder in this world are in a miserable condition; for where every object we behold, and every circumstance of our own being, and that of others, is, properly speaking, miraculous, who can survey them with indifference and feel no desire to penetrate into their mystery must be either mournfully dull by nature, or grievously blunted by use."

So, in the latter part of the year 1848, Mrs Crowe must have had every reason to feel pleased with herself. She was regarded as one of the leading women novelists of the time, and also held in respect as the champion of an attitude of scientific rationality in matters of the 'supernatural'. She was still only on the threshold of middle age and might have anticipated many more years of fame and success.

But fate was about to play an unkind trick on her. For it was in the year 1849 that the first rumours reached England of the latest craze to sweep America: Spiritualism. It had started in 1848 with strange rapping noises in the house of the Fox family in Hydesville, New York, and the two daughters of the house Margaretta and Kate, had discovered that they could communicate with the phantom rapper, who claimed to be a pedlar who had been murdered in the basement by a previous tenant. (Many years later, the collapse of a wall in this basement revealed a skeleton.) Soon people all over America were claiming to be able to communicate with 'spirits' and were holding 'seances'. In fact, 'table tuning' had been known since the beginning of the century; but the 'spirits' who communicated with the Fox sisters insisted that it should be regarded as the basis of a new religious revelation. The combination of 'mediumship' and Christianity proved irresistible, and by 1850 Spiritualism was as popular in England, France, Germany, and Russia as it had been in America.

Inevitably, there were many charlatans and tricksters among the 'mediums', and every time one of these was exposed the sceptical scientists, who viewed this tidal wave of 'superstitious credulity' with dismay, raised a shout of triumph and declared that from now on, surely, no one could be so foolish as to believe in spirits.

Mrs Crowe was caught in the tidal wave of mud that deluged many other serious investigators of the paranormal, including Baron Karl von Reichenbach, the discoverer of 'odic force', and J. R. Buchanan, the discoverer of 'psychometry'—the ability of certain 'sensitives' to read the history of an object by holding it in their hands. I have told the sad story elsewhere (in my *Psychic Detectives*) and shall not repeat it here. It is enough to say that Mrs Crowe's attempt to establish psychical research on a rational, scientific basis was swept away by the storm, so that although *The Night-Side of Nature* remained as popular as ever, it was widely dismissed by 'serious' people as credulous and uncritical.

Not that Mrs Crowe was forgotten. Her next novel, *Adventures of a Beauty*, was as good as ever, revealing the same remarkable ability to tell a gripping story and to weave a complicated but oddly plausible plot. (This one is about a farmer's daughter who marries the heir to an estate but omits to make sure the marriage is properly registered; so, when her husband vanishes, she has no means of proving her claim.) *Light and Darkness* (1852) and *Linny Lockwood* (1854) showed no diminution of her powers, but after the latter was a five-year silence, finally broken by a strange little book, a mere 143 pages, called *Spiritualism and the Age We Live In*. Those who rushed to buy it to discover Mrs Crowe's views on the new Spiritualism craze must have been puzzled and disappointed. The author of the *DNB* article refers to it as having "slight reference to the nominal subject, but evincing a morbid and despondent turn of mind". In fact, the real trouble with the book is that Mrs Crowe is so much on the defensive that she fails to commit herself to anything. She talks a great deal about God: "God makes no full revelations", "God's ways are not man's ways" But although she has some penetrating things to say about a new science of man's 'inner being', she never gets around to explaining her views on Spiritualism—although we can infer that she was more or less in favour. She seems to be repeating the basic argument of *The Night-Side of Nature*:

"Once more I assert that whether these manifestations are from heaven or hell, or whether they exist at all, is a question that we have every right to ask..."

She talks darkly about a divine fountain of grace that is cut off from those who are unwilling to receive it—presumably referring to the sceptics—and ends by denouncing those who try to forbid the souls who are committed to their charge from trying to recover their birth-right. It is all extremely obscure and suggests that somebody had been 'getting at' Mrs Crowe and making her feel very defensive.

Soon after this, according to the author of the *DNB* article, she had a violent but brief attack of insanity—presumably, he means what we would now call a nervous breakdown. Although she recovered and lived on for another sixteen years (she died in 1876), she published no more books. It would probably be true to say that she was finally silenced by the people who had come to regard her either as the mouthpiece of a new form of cranky irrationalism or those who regarded her as a servant of the devil. (In Scotland, this breed persisted long after it had died out in other parts of the world).

It is a sad story. But readers of *The Night-Side of Nature* will find no sign of paranoia or despondency. It is the work of a vigorous and healthy mind that has no patience with stupidity or dogmatism. Three and a half decades later, the Society for Psychical Research paid a kind of posthumous tribute to Mrs Crowe by tacitly adopting her aims and methods; but they took care not to mention her name. I doubt whether the modern reader will see any reason to share their inhibitions.

# 12

# Introduction: *Death-Bed Visions* (D60)

by Sir William Barrett
Wellingborough, Northants: Aquarian Press. 1986.

In 1874, a young professor of physics was visiting a friend in County Westmeath, Ireland. Their conversation turned upon the subject of hypnosis—or 'mesmerism', as it was popularly known—and the friend suggested that they should try the experiment of hypnotizing some of the children from the village. The professor, whose name was William Barrett, was intrigued and baffled by the results of these experiments. One little girl was able to feel and taste things the mesmerist was feeling and tasting. When the mesmerist placed his hand over a lighted lamp, the girl snatched her own hand away, as if in pain. When he tasted sugar, she smiled with pleasure; when he tasted salt, she grimaced.

Now according to the well-known sceptic Professor W. B. Carpenter, results like this could be explained by a certain 'heightened sensitivity' caused by the hypnosis. Carpenter thought that their hearing and sense of smell became so acute that they could sense what was being done behind their backs, but Barrett could see this was quite impossible: salt and sugar do not have any smell. Other experiments made the 'heightened sensitivity' theory quite unacceptable. A playing card was taken at random from a pack and placed in a book. The hypnotized girl held the book close to the side of her head, and correctly identified the card as the five of diamonds. In other experiments, another hypnotized person was able to tell the time on a watch that had been placed in a closed box, with its hands altered at random; another correctly identified fourteen cards taken at random from a pack.

For Barrett, these results were thoroughly disturbing. Science had always been the love of his life, and at nineteen, he had been the assistant of the famous physicist, and 'freethinker', Professor John Tyndall. Appointed to a professorship at the Royal College of Science in Dublin at the age of twenty-eight (in 1873), Barrett was fascinated by the phenomena of light and heat and made some important investigations into 'sensitive flames', as well as inventing two new alloys. As a friend and disciple of Tyndall, he might have been expected to march at the forefront of those common-sense men of science who detested the preposterous mumbo-jumbo called Spiritualism that had swept Europe and America since the 1850s. And now he was stumbling upon evidence that seemed to fly in the face of the basic tenets of modern science. But Barrett was an honest man. Instead of conveniently 'forgetting' about this baffling evidence—as some of his more distinguished contemporaries did—he wrote a paper about it, and in 1876, submitted it to the British Association for the Advancement of Science. Now it so happened that the chairman of the committee that vetted the papers was Alfred Russel Wallace, the naturalist who discovered evolution at the same time as Charles Darwin. Thirty years earlier, in the days when he was a schoolmaster, Wallace had conducted some almost identical experiments in hypnosis with his pupils. He had also discovered a boy who smiled with pleasure when he—Wallace—put sugar into his own mouth, and who snatched away his hand when he stuck a pin in his finger. So, Wallace approved the paper, in spite of protests from his colleagues, and it was read at Glasgow in 1876. But that was as far as the British Association would go, and the committee flatly refused to publish the paper. No doubt this wilful blindness on the part of his colleagues made Barrett more determined than ever not to be silenced. He began studying a new craze that was sweeping the drawing rooms of Great Britain in the

1870s—the 'willing game'. As in 'Hunt the Thimble', a person was sent out of the room, and the others then hid something—or decided on some action that the person should be 'willed' to perform, like scratching his nose or removing his glasses. It was often startlingly successful, and Barrett soon became aware that telepathy was involved. A Derbyshire clergyman, the Revd A. M. Creery, found that his daughters could guess the names of towns and people, even lines of poetry, when the others 'willed' them to. He contacted Barrett and Barrett was so impressed that he wrote a short report about it in *Nature* in 1881.

Staying with a friend in London that winter, Barrett raised the possibility of a founding a society of scientists and philosophers who would consider these strange phenomena with an open mind. The same idea had occurred to a distinguished Cambridge scholar, Frederick Myers, when he was taking a walk in the starlight with his old teacher, Professor Henry Sidgwick, in 1869. A 'Spiritualist Association' they had helped to found in the mid-1870s had not been very successful: respectable public figures were reluctant to be associated with Spiritualism. But when Barrett called a meeting in January 1882, he suggested that they should avoid being labelled Spiritualists and insist that they were simply a group of open-minded scientists who wanted to investigate unexplained phenomena. Nobody was very enthusiastic. All the same, Sidgwick reluctantly agreed to be president of this new association, and in the following month, the Society for Psychical Research was launched.

One of Barrett's first tasks was a new and more thorough investigation of the Creery children. Sidgwick, Myers, Edmund Gurney, Balfour Stewart, and Barrett himself went to enormous lengths to exclude fraud. The four girls were tested separately and together, and the results were impressive: in one test, the girl was able to guess correctly nine cards out of fourteen that were pulled randomly from a pack. (A statistician worked out that the odds against this were about nine billion billion billion billions.) In July 1882, Barrett published those results in the *Nineteenth Century* magazine commenting that surely nobody was going to accuse the experimenters of deliberate fraud. But in the next issue, someone did precisely that. A man called Horatio Donkin asked which was most likely, a nine billion billion billion billion to one chance or deliberate collusion between the children and the distinguished scientists? (This came to be known as 'Donkin's Law'.) Barrett was unconcerned. The Society had attracted some very distinguished members, including Gladstone, Lord Tennyson, Mark Twain, Lewis Carroll, John Ruskin, William James, and Alfred Russel Wallace himself. He felt—correctly—that he had finally turned paranormal investigation into a serious subject. No longer could sceptical scientists like Carpenter and Lankester dismiss the whole thing with an angry sneer.

The Society was to have many setbacks. Well-known mediums were caught cheating; others—like the remarkable Daniel Dunglas Home, who could make tables float up to the ceiling and wash his face in red hot coals—produced such astonishing results that no one believed them anyway. One problem was soon apparent: that 'psychical research' could never become an exact science because its experiments were not repeatable in the laboratory. Everything seemed to depend on the mood of the subjects. When the Creery children were happy and excited, they seldom made a mistake (they once guessed seventeen cards correctly one after the other); when they were 'playing' with dull or sceptical people, their performance dropped off. They were at their best when they were playing 'for fun' and felt that it didn't matter whether they succeeded or not. As soon as they felt things were getting too serious, they began to fail. Seven years after Barrett had first tested them, they were caught cheating. They admitted they had begun to use a code—coughs, slight movements, and so on—because they were afraid of disappointing people who had come to see them. They insisted that all their early results were genuine, and Barrett's reports make it almost certain they were telling the truth; but it was yet another blow to the Society for Psychical Research.

Barrett was dragged into belief in 'the paranormal' against his will—even against his better judgement. He was perfectly willing to believe in thought-transference (or telepathy, as Myers labelled it in 1882), but was inclined to believe that the kind of phenomena produced by Home—like floating out of one second storey window and in at another—were some kind of hallucination. But as some close personal friends, whom he could trust absolutely, developed powers of mediumship, he had to abandon that theory. Yet he still tried hard to find scientific explanations for the phenomena he was now witnessing every other day. As a scientist, he was impressed by the theory of the 'luminiferous ether'—the invisible fluid that is supposed to transmit light waves. It struck him that something of the sort might also explain hypnotism; that perhaps there was a 'magnetic fluid' that passed from the hypnotist to his subject, or some kind of 'psychic ether' that could carry mental 'waves'. When he became interested in dowsing, he decided that the explanation was probably 'electrical', some form of electric field associated with flowing water. But at the end of his classic book *The Divining Rod* (1926), written with Theodore Besterman, he has to admit that none of the 'physical theories' can explain all the phenomena that he tested—for example, the extraordinary fact that some dowsers can detect water by suspending a pendulum over a map—and that the likeliest explanation is that some unknown part of the mind causes the dowsing rod or pendulum to answer questions. Eventually, towards the end of his life, he admitted that his investigations had finally led him to believe in the existence of a 'spiritual world' and of life after death.

It is unfortunate that Barrett seems to have been such a modest man. Unlike many other eminent psychical investigators he never wrote an autobiography, so the details of his life have to be gleaned from comments by friends and colleagues. For some strange reason, there is no entry on him in the *Dictionary of National Biography*, and none in the *Encyclopaedia Britannica*. In order to write this introduction, I asked the help of the London Library, the Society for Psychical Research, and the College of Psychic Studies. They were able to send me almost nothing. When I told my wife how little I had been able to find out she said jokingly, 'Perhaps he didn't really exist', and there have been moments when I found myself starting to entertain this hypothesis. But a memoir published in the *Proceedings of the S.P.R.* by Eleanor Sidgwick shortly after Barrett's death mentions that he was a bachelor until 1916, living with a devoted sister who kept house for him. In 1916, he married 'the distinguished surgeon and gynaecologist' Mrs Florence Willie. And it is to the collaboration between the two that we owe his most fascinating and influential book, *Death-Bed Visions*.

In spite of its shortness, this is one of the most remarkable and original contributions to psychical research ever published. Barrett was interested in the fact that people on the point of death often seem to see dead relatives. This could easily be dismissed as hallucination, except that, in many cases, the dying person was unaware that the relative in question was already dead. The story of Jennie and Edith, recounted in Chapter Two, is typical. Two eight-year-old girls died in a diphtheria epidemic, one of them three days after the other; Edith was not told that Jennie was already dead. On the point of death, three days later, she apparently saw her friend walk into the room, and asked her father, 'Why did you not tell me that Jennie was here?'

The problem with this narrative is that it lacks detail, and although Barrett describes it as 'well authenticated', and cites the authority of Dr James Hyslop, a notoriously 'tough-minded' member of the American Society for Psychical Research (which, incidentally, was also founded by Barrett), most casual readers are bound to wonder whether it really happened. But when Barrett cites cases of which his own wife was a witness, then this objection vanishes. If we can trust Barrett, and the corroborative evidence that his wife collected from relatives and nursing staff, then we may assume that a 'death-bed vision' like the one described at the beginning of Chapter Two really took place exactly as described. Of course, that still does not prove that Mrs B. really saw her dead sister Vida. It could have been a hallucination. It is true that Mrs B. did not know that Vida was dead, but then, perhaps she guessed it from some hint dropped by her family or learnt of it by some other means. But hallucination or not, it offers a great deal of food for thought.

In fact, as we have already noted, this problem of life after death was the greatest stumbling block to those early members of the Society for Psychical Research. 'Spiritualism' originated around the year 1850 in Rochester, New York, as a result of a series of strange events that took place in the home of the Fox family, who lived in Hydesville—bangs and rapping noises that were soon being interpreted by means of an alphabetical code. The 'Spiritualist' movement soon spread across America, then to Europe. 'Mediums' began delivering messages from the dead, and scientists lost no time in denouncing the new craze as a delusion that could only appeal to the feeble-minded. One sad result of this wave of angry scepticism was that everyone who was interested in so-called paranormal faculties was tarred with the same brush. Hypnosis, telepathy, precognition, 'second sight', were all regarded with equal suspicion.

So, when Barrett succeeded in founding a society for the study of these dubious matters, he had performed a considerable service to the cause of paranormal research. During its early years, the Society for Psychical Research published important studies of telepathy, hallucinations, and 'phantasms of the living' (or *döppelgangers*). Many of its members—perhaps the majority—were disinclined to believe in life after death. Many of them agreed with Lewis Carroll, who wrote: "That trickery will *not* do as a complete explanation of all the phenomena I am more than convinced." And he went on to suggest "the existence of a natural force allied to electricity, by which brain can act on brain." To be a member of the S.P.R. was by no means synonymous with being a Spiritualist.

But the Society also accumulated an enormous body of well-authenticated testimony about 'ghosts' and spirits. While much of this could be dismissed as hallucination, or explained in terms of telepathy (for example, people who 'saw' relatives who had just died in some distant place), there was a small proportion of these cases that seemed to defy this kind of explanation. One single example will suffice. In 1921, a farmer named James Chaffin died in North Carolina, leaving the farm to his third son, Marshall, and nothing to his wife or other three sons. Four years later, his son James had a dream in which his father stood by his bedside, wearing an old black overcoat, and told him: "You will find my will in my overcoat pocket." Chaffin hurried to his mother, who told him that the overcoat had been given to his brother John. In John's house, they examined the coat, and found sewn into the lining a note saying, "Read the 27th chapter of Genesis in my daddy's old Bible". And in the 27th chapter of Genesis, there was another will, post-dating the one that left everything to Marshall and dividing the property between his wife and four sons. Marshall at first contested the case, but when he saw the will, he had to admit that it was genuine. The property was accordingly re-divided. A lawyer who investigated the case on behalf of the S.P.R. had no doubt that no deception was involved. In which case, it is hard to avoid the conclusion that old James Chaffin changed his mind during his last illness and inserted the new will in the Bible—probably convinced that it would be found soon after his death—then decided that he had to 'return' to draw his son's attention to it.

It was cases like this that finally convinced many members of the S.P.R. that life after death was not entirely a matter of wishful thinking. Both Sir Arthur Conan Doyle and Sir Oliver Lodge had been members of the S.P.R. since the 1890s without believing in life after death. Lodge was finally convinced after the death of his son Raymond in the First World War, when several mediums brought him messages that seemed to prove beyond all doubt that Raymond was still alive, while Doyle changed his mind when a young invalid who practised 'automatic writing' began to produce the handwriting of Doyle's brother-in-law—killed recently at Mons—and revealed a secret that was only known to himself and Doyle. Yet both Doyle and Lodge were violently attacked by sceptics for their 'credulity' and gullibility.

But of all the investigations initiated by those early members of the S.P.R., it was Barrett's research into 'death-bed visions' that was ultimately to bear the most rewarding fruit. The trouble with some of the most convincing 'evidence for survival' collected by the S.P.R. is that it is highly complicated. The 'Cross Correspondences' case is perhaps the most convincing in the whole literature of psychical research, for the 'spirits' apparently communicated through several mediums, and the messages were pieced together afterwards like a jigsaw puzzle; it is hard to think of a more convincing way of eliminating fraud, coincidence and pure wishful thinking. Yet a study of the complete evidence would take months (it runs to thousands of pages) and requires a knowledge of Greek, Latin, and several other languages.

But there is a satisfying feeling of common sense about Barrett's study of patients on the point of death. If a large percentage of the dying really *do* see dead relatives, then surely it should be perfectly easy to collect evidence?

During the 1930s and 40s, the Society for Psychical Research lost most of its original impetus; to begin with, it became dominated by sceptics, who became known as the 'High'n Dries', and who seemed to be convinced that the purpose of the S.P.R.

was to regard all 'paranormal occurrences' with deep suspicion. But in America, paranormal research was given new impetus by Dr J. B. Rhine, at Duke University, who decided that such matters as telepathy and psychokinesis could be investigated in the laboratory by statistical methods. One of this new breed of psychical researcher was Dr Karlis Osis, born in Riga, Latvia, in 1917, who worked with Rhine at Duke, and later became the research director at the Parapsychology Foundation in New York. Osis had the sensible idea of sending out a questionnaire to hundreds of doctors and nurses asking them about their own observations of dying patients. What interested Osis was what he called, from Keats' sonnet, 'Peak in Darien' experiences — with its suggestion of reverence and awe.

What he discovered was that fear is not the dominant emotion in dying patients, even children. A surprising number experienced elation and exaltation. About one in twenty had 'Peak in Darien' experiences, sometimes with visions of heaven. On one point, his findings differed from those of Barrett; not all 'death-bed visions' were of dead relatives: 52 per cent were of dead relatives, 28 per cent of relatives who were still alive and 20 per cent of religious figures like Jesus or the Virgin. On the other hand, the much earlier Census of Hallucinations taken by the Society for Psychical Research discovered that people in normal health saw twice as many living relatives as dead ones. So Osis's findings certainly indicated that dying people had at least reversed the 'normal' tendency. Moreover, these patients were not usually in a fever or in pain; they were fully awake and able to respond intelligently to questions. His general conclusion was that dying people feel no fear of dying, and often believe they are being met by dead relatives.

In fact, a mountain climber named Albert Heim had made a similar discovery in the 1870s. Heim had fallen seventy feet to a snow-covered ledge and had experienced a feeling that time had slowed down and a sense of 'divine calm'. He began to talk to other climbers who had had serious falls and found that these experiences were commonplace. All this led to the suggestion that perhaps people who are facing sudden, violent death may slip spontaneously into an ecstatic 'death trance', whose biological purpose is to remove the terror of death. In fact, one doctor made a similar suggestion about Osis's *Deathbed Observations by Physicians and Nurses*, pointing out that he himself had experienced a curiously ecstatic feeling when he came close to death by drowning, and also when his oxygen equipment in a high-flying plane froze up. Therefore, he suggested, 'death-bed visions' may be due to oxygen starvation. Osis countered this by pointing out that the visions often occurred in conscious patients long before the 'death coma'.

Another researcher, Erlendur Haraldsson, conducted research into death-bed visions in India, to see whether a totally different culture would have any effect on the 'near death experience'. He discovered that the answer was no. There was a remarkable similarity between the death-bed visions of Hindus and of Americans.

A similar set of observations was made by Dr Elizabeth Kübler-Ross, a European who had visited the death camps at the end of the war. When she married an American academic, she began to feel that America is a 'death denying culture' — that there is a deliberate attempt to ignore the reality of death. She gained considerable notoriety when she invited a girl dying of leukaemia to her classes in Chicago and confirmed that the experience was good for the girl *and* for the other students. Then Kübler-Ross began a systematic study of dying patients. Her observations, similar to those of Barrett and Osis, finally led her to a firm belief in life after death and in reincarnation. She came to believe that everyone has an unconscious knowledge of the time of their own death, and that all who die are met by dead relatives or other loved ones. Inevitably, her own emotional commitment has led to the accusation that her work is simply a tissue of wishful thinking. Yet it also has to be acknowledged that she has based her conclusions on hundreds of observations of the dying.

In the mid-1970s, Elizabeth Kübler-Ross was sent the proof of a little book called *Life After Life*, by a doctor called Raymond Moody, and her immediate comment was that she might have written it herself. Moody had become interested in 'near death' experiences as a student at the University of Virginia and had been collecting them for years without realizing that anyone else was doing so.

What interested Moody was that there was so much similarity between these cases. Again, and again, people who were on the point of death experienced the deep sense of peace and serenity described by Albert Heim. A very large number of them then found themselves moving through some kind of tunnel, usually with a light at the end. And in case after case, they found themselves standing outside their own bodies, often puzzled because other people in the room seemed unable to see them, and even walked right through them. Again, there were many glimpses of a 'heavenly realm', and the phrase 'city of light' occurred repeatedly. Patients often experienced a sudden flash of mystical revelation, an apparent glimpse into the meaning of life and the universe. Again, and again, they described a certain point at which they could make a choice: to go on and 'die', or to return to the world of the living. Many chose the latter alternative with great reluctance because they felt it was their duty to children or other living relatives. (And many people rescued from drowning have commented: 'I want to go back!')

Moody's book became an immediate best-seller and created a new academic industry, 'Near Death Studies'. Kenneth Ring, a professor of psychology at the University of Connecticut, attempted a far more comprehensive and systematic survey than Moody's; but he also reached the same general conclusions. In hundreds of cases of patients who had recovered from serious illnesses, and were believed to be dying, there were the same descriptions of the 'tunnel', the 'out of the body' experience, the sense of communication with benevolent beings ('guardian angels'), and the choice of death or a return to life. Others who have verified Ring's findings have been Michael Sabom, Edith Fiore, Maurice Rawlings, and Margot Grey. Margot Grey, an Englishwoman, was struck down by fever in India in 1976 and hovered between life and death for three weeks; she seemed to spend much of this time outside her own body, hovering near the ceiling and experiencing a pleasant sense of freedom. She has subsequently described her own researches into NDEs (near death experiences) in *Return From Death*, and has founded an International Association for Near Death Studies in Great Britain.

Do 'NDEs' *prove* life after death? Obviously not. They could be, as the sceptics insist, merely some kind of dream state. Yet Kenneth Ring, who admits that he has finally been convinced of the reality of 'survival', adds that the near death experience seems to him to be a kind of *teaching* experience: that even if it could be scientifically proved to be some form of hallucination, its value would still lie in its effect on those who experience it—a kind of 'bird's-eye view' of their own lives, and a certainty that life is not a 'tale told by an idiot', but has a meaning too profound to be grasped by our senses.

I have to admit that my own attitude to the question of 'survival' has always tended towards scepticism. As a child, I was much impressed by works like Sir Oliver Lodge's *Raymond*, and since my grandmother was a spiritualist, I heard a great deal about the subject of life after death. But when, at the age of about ten, I decided that I wanted to be a scientist I began to feel that my grandmother's beliefs were little more than wishful thinking. As it happened, I became a writer instead of a scientist, and in due course, was asked by a publisher to write a book on 'the occult'. When I settled down to a systematic study of the subject, I was finally forced to admit that so-called paranormal faculties like telepathy and clairvoyance are as well authenticated as 'perfect pitch' in a musician or the ability of aborigines to find underground water. Yet, on the whole, I preferred to maintain a sceptical attitude about such matters as life after death. It seemed clear to me that the 'poltergeist', or noisy ghost, is some kind of strange manifestation of the unconscious mind of a teenager—a view that was strengthened when I discovered 'split brain physiology' and learned that we literally have two different people living in the right and left hemispheres of the brain.

In 1980, I was asked to write a book on the poltergeist. And as soon as I began a careful, systematic study of the phenomena, from medieval Germany to modern Brazil, I found myself forced to face a highly disturbing conclusion: that the poltergeist is not some unexplainable freak of the divided brain, but is, just as our ancestors always believed, a spirit. I must admit that I reached this conclusion with deep reluctance, for I greatly prefer the 'scientific' theory about the unconscious and the split brain—which, from the point of view of psychical research, is far more respectable. But honesty compelled me to admit that it does not fit the facts as well as the 'spirit theory'. (I have explained precisely why in *Poltergeist!*.) Oddly enough, I still remained sceptical about 'life after death'. Or perhaps a better word would be 'agnostic'. I felt that far too much of the 'evidence' sounds like wishful thinking, and that although it is *possible* that we survive death, there is no actual case that strikes me as totally convincing.

In 1984, I began researching a book about life after death— which, again, had been commissioned by a publisher. And once again, the need to study an enormous amount of evidence in detail gave me a completely new perspective on the problem. Most of the 'evidence' I had known before, but piecemeal, as it were. Reading hundreds of cases, and then writing a book about it, finally convinced me that the evidence for 'survival' is very powerful indeed, and that if a scientist was faced with a similar weight of evidence for black holes or faster-than-light particles, he would regard their existence as scientifically proven. I am still not a 'spiritualist.' I do not attend seances, read spiritualist literature or play with a ouija board. Yet I feel reasonably certain that we somehow survive the death of the body.

This, of course, raises all kinds of difficult questions—such as what precisely happens to us after death, and what is the relation between the human personality and the physical body that seems so much a part of it. My theory about such matters is still extremely hazy. But I can at least outline the basic philosophy implied in the kind of evidence that Barrett provides in this volume. In fact, the essence of such a theory was already present in my first book *The Outsider*, written thirty years ago. In an essay on Bergson, T. E. Hulme suggested that, according to Bergson, 'life' is attempting to conquer, or force its way into, matter. So, the amoeba could be regarded as a very small 'leak', while a horse is a bigger 'leak' still, and man is the largest 'leak' so far.

Now when Bergson—and Shaw—proposed this idea, around the turn of the century, I think it unlikely that either of them thought of 'life' as an *intelligent* force. They thought of it, as Schopenhauer thought of the will, as a kind of 'blind striving'. This is because neither of them believed that intelligence—and personality—can exist apart from the physical body. But Bergson became increasingly interested in psychical research, and actually served for a time as president of the S.P.R.; it obviously struck him that *if* the human personality can exist apart from the physical body, then this implies that there is some other 'level' of existence—some other dimension, so to speak —where 'life' is not trapped and enclosed in matter as it is on our earth.

Madame Blavatsky had said something of the same sort.

She claimed that when the earth originated, it condensed out of some kind of gas that we would regard as completely 'non-material'. It is, she says, destined to pass through seven periods, or Rounds. We are now in the fourth, and this is the first Round that is solidly material. The fifth, sixth, and seventh rounds will once again be 'etherialized'. So, we are now trapped in the 'heaviest' level of existence. This makes life exceptionally difficult. But it also offers us more opportunities for creative activity than any previous race because the sheer 'solidness' of matter gives us something to brace ourselves against.

I am not, of course, suggesting that we should take Madame Blavatsky's cosmology too seriously. But her basic idea is roughly the same as Bergson's: that this material universe is only one level (or 'dimension') of reality, and that it is also the most 'solid' and difficult—so solid and difficult that the vital spirit finds itself in the same position as a man who happened to land on the surface of a planet a thousand times as large as ours: weighed down by an intolerable force of gravity that would make every movement an agonizing effort. On earth, the human spirit is like some expedition that has been sent to the Congo or the North Pole: living under conditions of incredible hardship, with almost no contact with 'base', and with the problem of conquering the environment until it can finally offer a foothold for civilization.

But our 'earth expedition' has a problem that is not usually encountered by explorers: amnesia. When a baby opens its eyes in its mother's arms it has already 'forgotten' its origin. And as we struggle to keep alive and to achieve some small degree of freedom, most of us quickly reach the conclusion that the world in which we find ourselves is 'all there is'. And this is perhaps the worst thing that can happen since it makes us virtually useless as explorers. If, having gone to the trouble of getting ourselves born in this remote and wearisome corner of the universe, we promptly forget why we came, we might as well pack up and go home....

So, whether or not we can accept the evidence presented by Barrett in this volume, we can at least gain a great deal of benefit by regarding it as symbolically true. Many people who have been through the 'near death experience' find that their view of their own lives has been completely transformed, and that they have ceased to regard life as brief, brutal, and pointless. If *Death-Bed Visions* can produce even a diluted version of this insight, then it undoubtedly deserves its place as one of the great classics of psychical research.

# 13

# Foreword: 'Visions and Veils.' *Secret Shrines: in Search of the Old Holy Wells of Cornwall* (D73)

by Paul Broadhurst
Launceston, Cornwall: Privately published, 1988.

In 1944, Robert Graves wrote a book of such apparently wild eccentricity that, in spite of his established reputation, it was turned down by a number of publishers, one of whom hinted, in a rejection letter, that Graves had gone off his head. *The White Goddess* was eventually accepted by T. S. Eliot and published in 1948 by Faber and Faber. The critics received it with bafflement. What were they to make of a book that argued that poetry came into existence in some remote 'Matriarchal age', when the Moon Goddess was the most powerful of all divinities, and that the human race has been going downhill ever since the priestess matriarchs were replaced by priest patriarchs? Was it a joke? Or perhaps an allegory? Or just an extraordinary piece of self-assertion by a paranoid poet? Graves records with satisfaction that one publisher who turned it down with particular rudeness was soon after found hanging in his garden, wearing ladies' underwear, while T. S. Eliot received a Nobel Prize and an O.M. in the same year....

In the forty years since its publication, the thesis of *The White Goddess* has been recognized as a profound insight into human history and human psychology. What Graves had understood was this: that the kind of knowledge taught in our universities is as crude and impersonal as a railway timetable. We have forgotten that there is a *totally different kind of knowledge*, and a totally different kind of knowing. And this was not just a cranky theory, but an intense conviction based on personal experience. One of Graves' fellow pupils at his public school was a boy called Smilley. One day, when the mathematics teacher had set them a complicated problem, Smilley had simply written down the answer; asked how he did it, Smilley replied "It just came to me." The master accused him of cheating and sent him to be caned. And eventually, Smilley was 'cured' of his odd ability to 'see' the answers to complex problems 'in a flash'. Graves knew Smilley's powers were genuine because he himself had had a brief experience of the same thing; one day, sitting on the grass-roller behind the cricket pavilion, he suddenly 'knew everything.' He explains (in the autobiographical story 'The Abominable Mr Gunn') that it was some kind of shift of awareness, an odd way of 'looking sideways' at disorderly facts to make order out of them. This 'mystical' way of seeing lasted about twenty-four hours, until he tried to explain it on paper; then it went. But Graves remarks that this insight was "a sudden infantile awareness of the power of intuition, the supra-logic that cuts out all the routine processes of thought and leaps straight from problem to answer." In *The White Goddess*, Graves calls this intuitive way of knowing 'lunar knowledge', and the kind of intellectual calculation taught at universities 'solar knowledge.' He has no deep objection to solar knowledge but feels that it is important for us to recognize that it is younger and cruder than 'lunar knowledge'.

In the mid-1960s, a scholar named John Michell stumbled on a series of discoveries that were closely related to Graves's insight. He discovered, to begin with, a little book called *Feng Shui* by the Rev. E. J. Eitel, about the ancient Chinese science of 'wind and water', whose purpose was to establish harmonious relations between people and their natural surroundings. In a reprint of Eitel's book, Michell remarked that "at the time Eitel was writing (1873), the triumph of materialistic philosophy and science...was so apparent that it was scarcely possible for a rational European to express any serious interest...in Feng-Shui." Yet, as Eitel records, the Chinese were amazed that the Europeans, so advanced in other respects, were ignorant of Feng-Shui, which they regarded as the foundation of civilized life. According to Feng-Shui, the earth is a dim mirror of the powers of heaven—another version of the old hermetic doctrine 'As above, so below'—and man must somehow 'open himself up' to these powers in the way that a great pianist must open himself up to the music if he wishes to express its very essence.

Michell also rediscovered the work of the retired English brewer Alfred Watkins: the notion that the network of footpaths and farm tracks that criss-cross rural England connect all kinds of 'sacred sites' such as churches, standing stones, ancient tumuli, and so on. Watkins believed they were the trade routes of ancient man, and that the men originally responsible for them were of priestly rank. Michell went further and suggested that these 'trade routes' were far more than that (as Watkins himself came to suspect at the end of his life)—that they were the 'lines of earth force' that the Chinese adepts of Feng-Shui called Lung Mei, or 'dragon paths'. Michell's book *The View Over Atlantis* (1972), although quietly received, was to become one of the most influential books of the decade, as well as a kind of Bible for intellectual hippies. The idea that had so much appeal to these heirs of the Beat Generation was that there must have been some remote time—symbolized by Atlantis—when man had a far more harmonious and direct relationship with nature—a kind of Golden Age. Paul Broadhurst expresses it (in Chapter Six of this book):

"In the early days of human development there seems to have existed a totally different relationship between the mind of man and its environment. The differentiation that clearly marks out the individual from his surroundings today was not so pronounced in those early times and man could feel the power of the essential 'one-ness' of things."

It would, I think, be a mistake to assume that stone age man went around embracing trees and gazing in rapture at the stars—he was too busy with the struggle to keep alive. But I believe it is also fairly certain—using the analogy of the modern primitives—that he used shamanistic magic in locating his prey, that he used natural powers of 'dowsing' to locate water, that he possessed the same powers of 'homing' as birds and animals, that he could 'tune in' to the weather and the seasons in a way that would nowadays be regarded as 'supernatural' (when, in fact, it is profoundly natural), and that he knew how to use the 'force' residing in standing stones and 'blind springs' for healing purposes.

It was in the 1960s that modern science stumbled upon what is almost certainly the true explanation of this paradox of 'lunar' and 'solar' knowledge. It happened when an American psychologist named Roger Sperry realized that man literally has two brains in his skull—or rather, that the human brain consists of two identical halves that can operate independently. The person you call 'I' lives in the left brain; the person who lives a few centimetres away is virtually a stranger.

It has been known for a long time that the left brain deals with language and logic, while the right deals with intuition and pattern-recognition—the left is a scientist, the right an artist or mystic. The 'you' is a scientist. Which explains why 'solar' (or scientific) knowledge comes naturally to us, while 'lunar' (or mystical) knowledge comes only in brief flashes. According to Robert Graves, our 'matriarchal' ancestors were 'right brainers'.

I apologize to readers to whom all this is familiar, but it can be seen that it forms a vital step in our argument—John Michell's and Paul Broadhurst's as well as mine. It demonstrates that civilized man has suppressed his 'intuitive' side until it is little more than a very faint voice on the telephone, instead of coming across loud and clear, as it did to our ancestors.

What *would* the world be like if we could somehow 'amplify' that lost faculty? Most of us glimpse the answer to that question in deep states of relaxation when the centre of gravity of consciousness seems to move to the 'right'. These are the states described, for example, by Wordsworth in *The Prelude*, when he tells how he rowed into the middle of lake Windermere at night, and how, looking at the vast shapes of the hills, he experienced a sense of *unknown modes of being*. In these mystical states, Wordsworth felt as if nature is *alive*. We take this to be merely a 'manner of speaking'—for, after all, a mountain is just a lot of dead rock—but if Graves (and Sperry) are correct, it could be far more than that.

There are still, in fact, many people who see the world as Wordsworth—or Graves' 'matriarchal primitives'—saw it. They are known as psychics or clairvoyants, and although the majority of scientists refuse to take them seriously, there has, in fact, been a great deal of scientific investigation of their powers. (See, for example, Lawrence LeShan's *The Medium, the Mystic and the Physicist*.) One of the most remarkable of these was a common-sense and down-to-earth lady called Rosalind Heywood, who was one of the most staunchly 'rationalistic' members of the Society for Psychical Research (until her recent death). Ever since childhood, Rosalind Heywood had been aware of 'presences' in nature, as well as of a 'presence' in her bedroom—she only learned later that two people in her family had seen the apparition of an old woman in there. As a nurse during the first world war, she became accustomed to curious intuitive promptings that enabled her to save lives, as well as to curious precognitions. Her autobiography *The Infinite Hive* is an immensely impressive book, because of its intelligence and honesty. And again, and again, she describes sudden powerful impressions of certain 'forces' in nature. There is, for example, the phenomenon she calls 'the Singing', "a kind of continuous vibrant inner *quasi*-sound, to which the nearest analogy is the noise induced by pressing a seashell against the ear", and which she was able to hear most strongly in lonely places such as open moorland—although she was aware of it to a lesser degree most of the time. Significantly enough, she also heard 'the Singing' in churches and libraries—anywhere where intense thought or worship had taken place. One day, she mentioned 'the Singing' to a young engineer, assuming he would pooh-pooh it; she was startled when he replied placidly: "Yes, I hear it too." (And only a few days ago, I received a letter from a correspondent named Peggy Brittain, who had read my account of Rosalind Heywood in my book *Afterlife*, and who wrote: "Rosalind Heywood's words (about 'the Singing') made me gasp with pleasure because this is something which I've experienced all my life, and haven't been able to find anyone else who seems to know what I'm talking about.")

What is so interesting is that Rosalind Heywood was able to hear it so clearly in old churches and libraries—as if these places had somehow recorded the feelings and thoughts that had taken place there over generations. It is also worth bearing in mind that—as Paul Broadhurst points out—many churches are built on the sites of 'pagan' temples or sites of worship, and these sites, in turn, were apparently chosen because of some powerful quality in the ground. It seems a logical inference that such places were chosen because the 'earth force' there was so strong and could therefore record and store up the religious emotion of worshippers, until the site had absorbed a certain sacred essence.

Guy Underwood, a remarkable dowser—who is quoted several times in this book—concluded that ancient monuments such as Stonehenge are built above 'blind springs' or aqua stats, so that the 'earth force' associated with them may be merely the 'magnetic' field of water. I mention this to emphasise that we are not now speaking of 'the occult' or supernatural, but simply about natural forces to which our ancestors were undoubtedly sensitive.

Having said that, it is necessary to admit that Rosalind Heywood herself finally became convinced—in spite of a fundamental tendency to scepticism—that not all 'psychic phenomena' can be explained by these more-or-less scientific terms. She describes, for example, how she and her husband arrived at Okehampton (in Devon) and went out to watch the sunset on the moor.

"Suddenly, without warning, the incredible beauty swept me through a barrier. I was no longer looking at Nature. Nature was looking at me.' And she did not like what she saw. 'It was a strange and humbling sensation, as if numberless unoffending creatures were shrinking back offended by our invasion...."

She found herself thinking "of the old days when simple souls linked themselves to wild nature by the ancient magic of oak and ash and thorn." They decided to stand still, and try explaining that they came as friends, with humility, only wanting permission to walk quietly on the moor. And almost immediately, both felt a sense of relief, as if they had been accepted.

Such an experience could have been totally subjective. But she was convinced that an experience two mornings later was not imagination.

"...I was alone by a window, facing the moor... Then I... suffered an invasion, a delightful one. It was as if, like ebullient children, a covey of little invisibles floated in at the window to say 'Hullo!' and coax me to play with them. For a moment their visit seemed perfectly natural, but then my analytical mind got going, and at once, for me, they ceased to exist...."

Did the "covey of little invisibles" exist in any objective sense? Rosalind Heywood insists that she keeps an open mind on the subject. But I personally have no doubt whatever that, in a relaxed 'right brain' state, she *perceived* 'unknown modes of being' just as Wordsworth perceived them.

It seems to me that there is an important lesson to be learnt from all this. In our ancestors, 'lunar' perception was as strong as—perhaps stronger than—'solar' perception. In the course of creating civilization, we have suppressed these 'right brain' perceptions. Yet I would suggest that, in a sense, we still have an important advantage over our ancestors. Our left-brains have developed an analytical power and force that would have struck them as rather repellent, just as most schoolchildren find the idea of quantum physics or symbolic logic repellent. Yet although we have suppressed our 'lunar' perceptions, we have not destroyed them; we can recover them by learning to 'relax into the right brain.' And this, in a fundamental sense, is what this present book is about. Paul Broadhurst is arguing that the 'healing power' that Matthew Arnold found in the poetry of Wordsworth also resides in the 'secret shrines' that so fascinate him, and that if a man of the 20th century should wish to learn about these deep forces of the human psyche and the natural world—and about the link between them—then he might find that the 'elementals' of such places make admirable tutors.

I have reason to believe him correct. It was just over thirty years ago—in 1957—that I began to find myself depressed and confused by my life as a writer in London, and by the exhausting persistence of journalists who had discovered that the so-called 'Angry Young Men' made good copy. After a preposterous scandal involving my girlfriend's parents—who arrived at my flat with a horsewhip and were soon followed by hordes of reporters and photographers—I took the advice of my publisher, and decided to leave London. It so happened that a poet who lived in the next room had a cottage in Cornwall, which he offered to let to us for an absurdly low rent. We moved there in the spring of 1957 and have been here ever since.

I realize now what an incredible piece of good luck it was that my friend happened to have a cottage in Cornwall—and not, say, Durham, which I would have accepted just as readily. Even now, Cornwall has not quite emerged from the 19th century, and the majority of its small villages have hardly changed since the time of Shakespeare. But the real magic of Cornwall resides in those places that never change—in the moors and the cliffs and the rocky inlets. Every afternoon, I work until 3 o'clock, until my brain seems to have lost its power to make intuitive leaps, then drive a mile to the clifftop, and walk along a footpath that has an almost continuous view of the coast from Plymouth to the Fal Estuary and the Lizard. And as I walk, I allow the empty sea and the unchanging landscape to soothe me into a state of quiescence. When this happens, it is as if some invisible wall dissolves away, and I catch a glimpse of a mode of existence that is completely foreign to flesh and blood, yet which seems to possess its own alien form of awareness. Words and images can never capture this mode of existence, but they can acknowledge its reality. The words and images that follow are an acknowledgement of this magical reality.

# 14

## Introduction: *Finding Your Guardian Spirit: the Secrets of Life After Death Revealed by Japan's Foremost Psychic* (D89)

by Aiko Gibo
New York: Kodansha International, 1992.

In February 1992, I was asked by a Japanese television company if I would be willing to make a programme with a Japanese psychic named Aiko Gibo. She was, they explained, one of the best-known psychics in Japan, and was at present traveling around the world with a television team, making a documentary to demonstrate her powers. And could I, they asked, suggest a haunted house in England where I might interview Mrs Gibo? I suggested a number of haunted houses, but the one the company chose was, in fact, a haunted pub in Croydon, South London. This pleased me, because I had already conducted an investigation into the pub—the King's Cellars—and written about it in my book *Poltergeist!*.

In 1980, when I was researching the book, I heard about the King's Cellars in Croydon, where a poltergeist smashed bottles and glasses and sometimes caused the lavatory to flush when there was no one present. On a visit to the pub, I saw this happen. But then, poltergeist hauntings seldom last for more than a few months—a year at the most. Therefore, I was surprised to hear recently that the Croydon poltergeist was still active. This is why I immediately suggested the Croydon pub when I was asked to interview Mrs Gibo.

On Sunday March 1, I waited in a hotel in central London for the arrival of the television team. They arrived about midday, and I was introduced to Mrs Gibo. I was pleasantly surprised.

For some odd reason, few mediums are physically attractive—to begin with, contact with spirits often seems to make them extremely fat. Aiko Gibo was an attractive woman who radiated good humour and vitality, and who also spoke excellent English. And as we waited for the producer, Mrs Gibo told me how she had become a medium.

As a child, she explained, she had been silent and introverted. One of her few close friends was a pretty little girl called Ayako, with whom she often played after school. When Ayako died suddenly, at the age of six, Aiko was stunned with sorrow. She became even more withdrawn. Then one day, as she was playing alone, she heard Ayako's voice saying: "What are you doing?" And suddenly, Ayako was in the room with her.

With the naturalness of a child, Aiko accepted this strange phenomenon; it merely proved what she had always sensed: that people do not die. She became accustomed to holding conversations with Ayako, and soon discovered that her friend could foresee the future. Ayako told her that on the following day, a man would be drowned in the river. The next day, it happened, just as Ayako had foretold.

Understandably, her mother and father were deeply disturbed that their daughter was so unlike other children, and they discouraged her from talking about her strange experiences. So, Aiko learned to keep silent about them. Her parents would have preferred her to be normal. As Aiko reached her late teens, they had their wish. Like any teenager she wanted to enjoy life and meet people. As she became more absorbed in everyday reality, her psychic powers gradually faded away.

She married a businessman, and the hard work of looking after a husband and bringing up three children turned her into a realist, who had no time for the world of the unseen. From the age of 21 to the age of 37, she had no further psychic experiences. Then, one day, it all came back. Her youngest son was four years old and had started in kindergarten. And one day, as she was having tea with a friend named Mrs Hayakawa, she suddenly "saw" Mrs Hayakawa's town, which was three hundred kilometres away. She also saw a graveyard in which one of the gravestones had fallen down and became aware of an old man with a long white beard, dressed in a kimono, who was complaining that his grave was being allowed to fall into disrepair. She described the graveyard and the old man to Mrs Hayakawa, who said with astonishment, "That sounds like my grandfather." But as far as she knew, the grave was in a good state of repair. Mrs Hayakawa telephoned her brother, who lived very close to the graveyard. Soon, her brother rang back to say that their grandfather's gravestone had been torn out of the ground, apparently by a vandal.

That night, Mrs Hayakawa dreamed of her grandfather, who was very angry. But when the grave was restored to its former state, Mrs Gibo became aware that the grandfather was now satisfied; his spirit was again at peace. When Mrs Gibo told her mother that her psychic powers had returned, her mother groaned, "Oh no!" and refused to speak to her for three days. At this point in her story, Mrs Gibo was interrupted by the arrival of the producer, and we went to eat a light lunch. Later that afternoon, a bus took us all to Croydon to visit the King's Cellars.

In fact, the pub had now changed its name, and was called Goody's. Since it was a Sunday, it was closed. The haunted bar is in the basement, and the landlady, a pretty girl called Tracy, took us down there.

As soon as we began to descend the stairs, Mrs Gibo stopped and said, "I can see a man lying at the foot of the stairs." Now in fact, I had earlier broken one of the first rules of psychical research and told Mrs Gibo that a landlord had been found dead at the foot of the stairs. Therefore, I realized, her vision could not be regarded as valid evidence.

As we reached the bar Mrs Gibo stopped again and stared. "A

girl has just walked across the room and disappeared through that wall." I asked her to describe exactly where the girl had come from, and she pointed to a wall behind the bar. I went behind the bar to see whether there had perhaps been a door there at some stage, but it was obvious that there had always been a wall.

I interviewed Mrs Gibo in front of the camera, after which I interviewed Tracy, the landlady, behind the bar. She told me that the poltergeist was still active—glasses often fell off the counter and broke, and on one occasion, the beer pump had begun to operate on its own, pouring beer over the floor.

At this point, the camera stopped to change film. I stood alone behind the bar, talking to Tracy. By this time, I must confess that my natural scepticism was in the ascendant, and I was beginning to feel that the whole thing was a waste of time. While I had no doubt that Mrs Gibo was sincere, I was beginning to wonder whether she was not allowing her imagination to be influenced by what I had told her. After all, it is extremely unusual for a poltergeist haunting to last for ten years.

As I stood talking to Tracy there was a loud clink from behind me. I turned round and saw that a heavy glass had fallen onto the floor. For a moment, I assumed that I had caught it with my coat. Then I realized that it was too far away for that. The glasses, which stood on a ledge beneath the counter, were at least three feet away. And we were quite alone—there was no one behind the bar with us, and no one who could have reached over from the other side. Suddenly, with astonishment, I realized that the poltergeist was showing me that it existed.

I quickly called to the producer, and the camera filmed me picking up the glass. Meanwhile, a fellow researcher named Maurice Grosse, an investigator from the Society for Psychical Research, explained that he had seen the glass fall off the shelf as if it had been pushed. He had been standing at the far end of the bar drinking a glass of wine and could see past me as the glass moved on its own.

I turned and bowed to the empty spot where the glass had fallen, saying, "Thank you." Suddenly, my scepticism had vanished.

Ten minutes later, when we had finished filming, I went across to the bar for another glass of wine. Tracy now stood talking to a woman friend, and as I listened to her conversation, I realized they were talking about the dead landlord. I had been unable to find any information about this landlord—even his name—and so had referred to him in *Poltergeist!* simply as the landlord. Now I heard Tracy refer to him as 'Bernard', and I asked her how she had learned his name.

It seemed that it had happened by chance. A week earlier, the fire extinguisher had gone wrong. A label on the extinguisher gave the address of the firm that maintained it. When Tracy telephoned them, and gave her address, the girl at the other end of the line said, "That used to be the King's Cellars, didn't it? I used to work there in the sixties." Tracy then asked if the girl knew anything about the ghost. "It was a landlord called Bernard. He came in late one Sunday night, very drunk, and fell downstairs. He was found the next morning with his neck broken." Tracy then asked if there were supposed to be any more ghosts. "Yes, there's a girl who committed suicide. She had quarrelled with her boyfriend in the pub and went back to work in the building next door. Later that day she threw herself off the roof. She landed on the roof of the pub and died."

I was excited and rushed to tell the producer what I had just learned. Not only had we found the name of the dead landlord, but also something about the girl Aiko Gibo had seen. Moreover, we had a witness who had worked in the pub at the time, and who could tell her story on camera.

An hour later, Mrs Gibo and I returned to our hotel, while the intrepid camera crew prepared to stay awake all night in the bar to film any manifestations that might occur. Knowing that poltergeists are notoriously camera-shy, I felt they were probably wasting their time. In fact, the next morning, they returned to the hotel, tired and disappointed. The poltergeist had, as I expected, declined to perform.

But I, at least, had been offered proof of the poltergeist—and of the remarkable powers of Aiko Gibo.

# 15

# Introduction: *The Goblin Universe* (D62)

by Ted Holiday
St Paul: Llewellyn Press, 1986.

About two years before his death, Ted Holiday sent me the typescript of his book *The Goblin Universe* and asked me for comments. I read it straight through in one sitting, and told him I thought it was excellent, and that I would be happy to recommend it to my publisher. Several months went by, and I had no reply. Then, to my surprise, he wrote saying that he was dissatisfied with the book and had decided to scrap it and write another. He never explained exactly why he came to dislike it. After his death, I contacted his mother, and asked her whether Ted had left another typescript behind, and if so, whether I could see it. When a parcel arrived from her a few days later, I tore it open eagerly—and discovered, to my disappointment, that it was the typescript of a book about lake monsters. It contained much important and fascinating material, but simply lacked the daring range and sweep of *The Goblin Universe*. And that is why I am now delighted to be able—with the permission of Mrs Florence Holiday—to offer *The Goblin Universe* to the American reading public.

As this book demonstrates, Frederick William Holiday (he acquired the nickname Ted in the RAF) was a highly original mind. He was also a countryman with a passion for fly fishing. And it was this passion, rather than a rather vague interest in the 'supernatural', that launched him on his career as investigator of the unknown. In August 1962, he drove in a light van to the shores of Loch Ness, equipped with fishing rods, a sleeping bag, and a camera. Ted had been twelve years old in 1933, when the new road was completed along the shores of Loch Ness, and the first sightings of the 'monster' were reported. He had always been fascinated by the mystery, so the trip to Scotland had a dual purpose.

That first evening, as darkness settled over the Great Glen, Holiday experienced an odd kind of nervousness. This was not the subjective reaction of a highly strung temperament, for this particular countryman had spent many a night in the open. He says:

"After sunset, Loch Ness is not a water by which to linger. The feeling is hard to define and impossible to explain.... Our genes have come down over a million years, from hutments and lake-dwellings, from dark gorges and cold caves. The seed of man's deepest instincts was planted sometime before the Pleistocene; our subconscious has accumulated many strange impressions and none of these can be gainsaid. After dark I felt that Loch Ness was better left alone."

That night was peaceful, but the next night, he woke up at midnight, when the Glen was totally silent, and was puzzled to hear the sound of waves crashing on the nearby beach. There was no sound of a boat out on the Loch—in any case, navigation is forbidden at night. But whatever was causing the continuous sound of waves must have been fairly large. Two days later, he was up at dawn, standing on a hillside with his binoculars in his hand; about 6 a.m. he had his first sighting of the monster. Something black and glistening and rounded appeared above the surface, projecting about three feet. Then it dived, producing an upsurge of water like a diving hippopotamus. Through his binoculars he could make out the shape below the surface— thick in the middle and tapering towards its extremities. It was blackish-grey in colour. Holiday guessed it to be between forty and forty-five feet long. He stood watching it for several minutes. Then, on a nearby pier, a workman began hammering on metal, and the monster vanished instantly.

That was the last time Holiday sighted the monster in 1962—and, in spite of hundreds of hours of watching, the last time he sighted it until 1965, when he saw it on two more occasions, on the first of which he watched it—looking like an upturned boat—from three different positions, racing his car along the shores of the loch to get a better view. But after that first sighting, he felt relatively sure that what he had been watching was simply a giant version of the common garden slug, an ancestor of the squid and the octopus. Like the octopus, he thought, the monster could probably change colour. He embodied these ideas in a paper and sent out forty copies to zoologists all over the country; most of them did not even acknowledge it. One 'expert' who allowed himself to be drawn into correspondence insisted that what most people have mistaken for the monster is a mat of gas-filled vegetation. But Ted Holiday had seen it, and he knew it was nothing of the sort. He studied every record he could find about 'worms' (a name that used to be applied to dragons; another variant is 'orm'), and discovered that there had been hundreds of sightings over the centuries, many of them on land. And finally, he set down all his theories in his first book, *The Great Orm of Loch Ness*, which appeared in 1968. His main argument is that the monster is a variety of giant slug, *Tullimonstrum gregarium*, a creature looking a little like a submarine with a broad tail, and that these monsters were once altogether more plentiful in England—hence the legends of the dragon. But the last chapter of his book offers a hint of another theory that was striving to surface from his subconscious mind. He speaks about the dragon-like fourth beast in the Book of Revelation and points out how often the dragon is regarded as a symbol of evil.... But this is merely a hint, and I may even be allowing my knowledge of his later work to influence my reading of the text.

Even at this stage, when he was convinced that the monster was merely a prehistoric survival, like the coelocanth, he was intrigued by one aspect of this elusive creature's behaviour: its apparent camera-shyness. Holiday himself had failed consistently to get a photograph—on one occasion his finger was on the button when the hump submerged. And other 'watchers' had experienced the same thing. They always seemed to get their best views of the monster when they had left the camera behind. It was possible, of course, that the creature was telepathic—as I believe many animals are—and could somehow sense the excitement of photographers. But Holiday found himself toying with Jung's idea of synchronicity, a suspicion that deepened after an odd little coincidence in 1971. In 1899, the tenant of Boleskine House, facing Loch Ness, had been the notorious 'magician' Aleister Crowley, who was then in his early twenties. Crowley believed that he was a reincarnation of Edward Kelley, the 'magical assistant' of the Elizabethan alchemist John Dee. Crowley had found Dee's own copy of a famous magical ritual by a certain Abramelin the Mage, and he set out to perform it at Boleskine. But the complete ritual takes about eighteen months to perform, and for some reason, he never completed it. He was apparently successful to the extent of conjuring up a number of shadowy figures—'demons' or spirits—and these seem to have caused a great deal of trouble—such as driving the coachman to drink and causing a clairvoyant to become a prostitute. According to Holiday: "From this point, misfortune stalked him everywhere"—although readers of John Symonds' biography of Crowley, *The Great Beast*, may feel this is a pardonable exaggeration, since Crowley spent the next few years wandering around the world and staying in the best hotels.

In 1969, American students exploring the cemetery near Boleskine House found a tapestry below a grave-slab. The tapestry was embroidered with humped, worm-like creatures;

it was wrapped around a large conch shell, which gave forth a braying sound when blown. They were fairly obviously ritual objects, of the kind used in magical ceremonies, and the dryness of the tapestry, and its freedom from mildew, suggested that it had only been hidden below the grave-slab for a day or two. The evidence suggested that someone had been engaged in a magical ceremony in the churchyard when they had been interrupted and had thrust the ritual objects under the grave-slab, where they were found accidentally before the owner could return for them. Soon afterwards, Ted was invited to dinner by a friend who lived close to the Loch; his fellow guest was an American named Dr Dee. Dr Dee, it turned out, was in England checking on his family tree, and he had discovered that he was a descendant of the Elizabethan magician. He was in Scotland by pure chance—Ted's friend had written to the Chicago Adventurer's Club about testing sonar equipment on Lake Michigan and had been put in touch with Dr Dee.

In 1971, there was another coincidence. As Ted was staring across the Loch, he found himself looking at the word DEE in large yellow letters. Bulldozers engaged in widening the road had scraped at the slope running down to the loch. But the letters—formed by the yellow sub-soil—were only half complete. Reflected in the mirror-like calm of the water, they formed the word DEE.

By this time, Holiday's investigations had already taken a new turn. In 1968, he had had his last sighting of the Loch Ness monster, ploughing across the lake; several people who were with him also saw it, but while he was running for his camera, it vanished under the surface. Later the same year, he heard of a report of a monster in a small lough (the Irish version of a loch) near Claddaghduff, in Galway. But when Ted went to Lough Fadda, he was puzzled that it seemed too small to house a monster; a fifteen foot 'pieste' (as the Irish call them) would soon eat all the fish and die of starvation. Yet when he spoke to witnesses, and studied accounts of other sightings in Ireland, it seemed clear that the sightings were genuine; on one occasion, the witnesses were two priests, on another, a middle-aged librarian. Such people would hardly be likely to invent a monster-sighting to gain notoriety. Besides, there are simply too many stories about lake monsters for them all to be invention. In the early 19th century, Thomas Croker collected many of them, which he published in a book of Irish legends. He sent this to Sir Walter Scott, who replied that many people near Abbotsford—where he lived—swore to having seen a 'water-bull' emerge from a lake hardly large enough to have held him. An Irish woman who saw one described it as having a head like a horse and a tail like an eel and called it a horse-eel. But dozens of descriptions make it clear that the Irish lake monsters belong to the same family as the Loch Ness monster.

Holiday decided to set up nets in a small lake called Lough Nahooin where a 'water horse' had been sighted. Something disturbed the nets; but there was no evidence that it was a lake monster. But Ted encountered another odd coincidence. While he was near the lough, he had neuralgic pains in his jaws which made sleep impossible, and they came and went over many days; his companion also suffered from them. Later, reading the *Egyptian Book of the Dead*, he came across a description of a 'Worm' of the marshes, and the worm is made to ask the goddess Ea (which signifies 'antelope of the deep') if he can "drink among the teeth, and...devour the blood of the teeth and of their gums...."

Although he does not say so, I think we may infer—from the number of times he mentions him—that Ted was reading a great deal of Jung at this time. Now as we know, Jung wrote a book on the 'Flying Saucer' phenomenon, in which he advanced the theory that Unidentified Flying Objects are not objectively real but are 'projections' of the human mind. Jung did not mean they were illusions—like the pink elephants seen by a dipsomaniac—but that they were, in effect, 'monsters from the unconscious' which had somehow managed to clamber out into the real world. Jung thought that they were modern man's religious symbols, or rather, his substitute for religious symbols. "The soul has a religious function," says Jung, meaning that man has an appetite for religious meaning which is exactly like his body's needs for vitamins. If he lives a life without real purpose, this function becomes starved, and he begins to experience a sense of boredom and futility. Then, Jung thought, he may begin to see certain 'archetypal' religious symbols floating around in the sky—his soul's attempt to remind him that something is missing. (But towards the end of his life, Jung apparently abandoned this belief—according to his niece—and came to admit that Flying Saucers may be as 'objectively real' as meteors).

Ted had himself seen a number of Unidentified Flying Objects—as described in the present book—and was apparently much taken with Jung's theory. But if a Flying Saucer can be a 'projection' of man's basic craving for 'goodness', then was it not just as conceivable that lake monsters are a projection of man's religious sense of evil? After all, the dragon was an ancient symbol of wickedness—hence the legend of St. George. And if Holiday was correct in his original assumption that dragons, 'worms' and lake monsters are the same thing, then the Loch Ness monster might be as unreal—objectively speaking—as the Jungian Flying Saucer....

Now the most interesting thing about Ted Holiday—and the most admirable—was his intellectual courage. When he encountered a mystery, he was perfectly capable of diving straight into it, and trying to swim down to the bottom. After ten years or so of investigating lake monsters, he was coming to the conclusion that they may be far more than prehistoric survivals. His encounters with 'ghosts'—also described in this book—had convinced him that 'there are more things in heaven and earth....' Now he began to toy with the idea that there may be some 'Jungian' connection between the deep realities of the human psyche and the elusive mystery of lake monsters and Flying Saucers. So, he embarked on a wide-ranging study of the literature of the past, in an attempt to trace a connection between UFOs, lake monsters and ancient religious symbols. He turned his attention to archaeology and was intrigued by the mystery of the barrows. There seem to be two types of barrows—or burial mounds: long barrows and round barrows, (or disc barrows). Most of them date from the Bronze Age. Many barrows contain ritual objects in the shape of discs— presumably, sun-discs. Holiday looked at aerial photographs of disc barrows—for example, at Winterbourne Stoke, near Stonehenge—and was struck by their resemblance to certain well-known Flying Saucer photographs. And in *The Dragon and the Disc* (1973), he boldly proposed the theory that the 'barrow culture' was, in effect, a Flying Saucer culture: that the builders of these great mounds were imitating objects they had seen in the sky. Holiday noted that many UFO sightings include 'cigar-shaped' objects, and that some people claim to have seen the smaller 'Flying Saucers' emerging from the cigar-shaped objects. The long barrows, he suggested, were based on the cigar-shaped UFOs.

There is, of course, a certain danger in constructing theories like these—a danger that can be seen very clearly in the work of Erich von Däniken. Däniken, as everyone knows, took up the extraordinary theories about UFOs suggested by Louis Pauwels and Jacques Bergier in their best-selling book *The Morning of the Magicians*, which appeared in 1960, and expanded them into an exciting theory about 'ancient astronauts', propounded in his immensely popular *Chariots of the Gods?* in 1967. But as soon as serious scholars began to examine Däniken's book, they became aware that he had an unfortunate tendency to distort the facts to fit his theories. One particularly notorious example is the photograph of something which Däniken alleges to be a 'parking bay' for an ancient spaceship—part of the famous Nazca lines in Peru. In fact, the 'parking bay' is the leg joint of a vast bird drawn on the surface of the desert, and is not more than a dozen feet in diameter—hardly large enough to park a car, still less a spaceship. Däniken hastened to explain that he was not responsible for the photograph or the caption—they had been inserted by an editor. Yet the photograph can still be seen in edition after edition of *Chariots of the Gods*; Däniken is apparently happy to allow the error to stand. Dozens of similar 'errors' could be cited. But the deathblow to Däniken's credibility was struck by the affair of the underground caves, described at the beginning of *Gold of the Gods*. Däniken alleged that he had visited these caves in South America and had seen amazing underground libraries engraved on sheets of metal; later he was compelled to admit that he had not actually been inside the caves, and that his account should be regarded as a kind of fiction. The 'library', of course, was pure invention.

This is the kind of problem that can easily arise when a writer becomes obsessed by a theory and determines to prove it at any cost. Holiday, fortunately, was not prone to that kind of 'enthusiasm'. His books exude an air of pragmatism and common sense. His temperament was altogether closer to that of another British student of the paranormal, the late Tom Lethbridge.[1] Ted Holiday was not quite so consistent a thinker as Lethbridge, but he possessed many of the same qualities, and his books impress for the same reason: because the reader feels he is speaking from personal experience.

Because he died in 1979, eight years after Lethbridge, Holiday was able to become acquainted with the notion of lines of 'earth force', known as leys, which had been made popular by the English scholar John Michell in the late 1960s. Michell was fascinated by the religious observances of the ancient world, as well as by the UFO phenomenon. And in his first book, *The Flying Saucer Vision*, (1967) Michell observed that "It is remarkable to what extent the flying saucer legend has incorporated former beliefs and superstitions, some of which were apparently moribund, and others embedded for centuries in Christian mythology." He also observed that

"The evidence... is that throughout its post-war history the flying saucer phenomenon and its literature have been associated with a change in prevailing modes of thought so radical that it amounts to a change in the popular cosmology; that is, the way people understand the universe and their place in it."

Michell pointed out that this supports Jung's view that UFOs are a portent of "long-lasting transformations of the collective psyche."

Ted Holiday came upon ley lines as a result of his study of bronze age archaeology. Lake monsters and UFOs had become connected in his mind as two mysteries of which he had some personal experience. In studying the ancient history of 'worms' and dragons, he came across many 'serpent carvings' in Christian churches, and on Celtic and Norse artefacts. But he also noticed carvings that bore a remarkable resemblance to Flying Saucers. So, like Däniken, Michell and Lethbridge, he found himself speculating whether our remote ancestors may have been acquainted with 'spacemen'. In *The Flying Saucer Vision*, John Michell had stated flatly that:

"...since (dragons) appear to be identical with the western concept of flying saucers...the discovery that dragons move over the earth's surface on certain straight lines will encourage those who are working to compare leys with the routes of flying saucers."

Michell was unaware at this early date that Chinese 'dragon paths' are crooked.

Holiday was more cautious; he simply felt that ancient symbolism seems to indicate some connection between dragons (or worms) and 'discs'. And in *The Dragon and the Disc*, he went a step further and suggested that Egyptian and Sumerian pyramids were, like Bronze Age disc mounds, "... response to the phenomena today called UFOs." What he seems to mean is that the pyramids embodied a knowledge of the universe—for example, the exact size of the earth—that was far beyond the science of their time.

In *The Flying Saucer Vision*, John Michell had already outlined his own controversial theory of the nature of UFOs.

"Hitherto all the theories of modern scholarship have, as Lenin observed, been based on the assumption that we are alone in the universe. The possibility that our whole development has been influenced by extra-terrestrial forces, with which we may again have to reckon sometime in the future, is hardly considered. Yet, as we have seen, this idea lay behind all the study and religious observances of antiquity. Our disregard for life outside the earth is something new, an attitude which we may not be able for much longer to maintain...."

This leaves us with an interesting question. Have the 'extra-terrestrials' set out to remind us of their existence with this new wave of Flying Saucers? Or do Flying Saucers originate in the 'collective unconscious' of the human race—in which case, we must suppose that the collective unconscious is trying to remind us of certain truths we have forgotten? Michell leaves the question open; he is far more concerned to remind his readers of 'the Flying Saucer vision', the vision of man as a part of a far wider universe. And in his second book, *The View*

*Over Atlantis* (1969) the 'Flying Saucer vision' has become the 'ancient knowledge system' that lies behind the Chinese science of *feng shui*—the recognition of the earth as a living body—while Atlantis has become the symbol of a remote Golden Age in which science was based on this recognition.

Holiday was also moving towards the view that both 'dragons' and Flying Saucers may be symbols—or perhaps a better word would be 'signals'—that is to say, that their purpose may be to 'remind' human beings that reality is altogether stranger and more complex than they think. The question of precisely who is making the signals is left open. But in the twelfth chapter of *The Dragon and the Disc*, he admits that:

"...by 1970 I had rejected the superficial view of monster phenomena—that they are just unknown animals that have somehow escaped the science net—as inadequate."

And he goes on to cite references in Celtic literature to the idea that the 'Serpent' is an apparition or phantom. And he goes on to suggest that in the ancient world the 'Disc' may have been worshipped in many places, while the dragon was worshipped by other groups. Such groups would today be called Satanists. He points out that Irish churches seem to lack the serpent designs found in so many English churches and suggests that perhaps this is what is meant by the legend that St. Patrick banished the serpents from Ireland—that he destroyed the ancient religion of dragon-worship.

And it is at this late point in *The Dragon and the Disc* that he goes on to speak about Aleister Crowley, and his Abramelin ritual at Boleskine House. He is already beginning to speculate that the phenomena he has been discussing may have something in common with what is traditionally called magic. In a final chapter, 'An Exercise in Speculation', he makes a heroic effort to pull together the various threads of the book, but it is well-nigh an impossibility. He speaks about 'other dimensions', and parallel universes, and points out that in many reports of UFOs, the object seemed to come and go, materialising and dematerialising moment by moment. Then he goes on to mention some of the odd phenomena observed in the Warminster area—a centre for ley lines as well as Flying Saucers—for example, the case of a couple who were driving home late at night when they saw a corpse lying with its feet in the road; when they stopped the car, it had vanished. But he is obviously not sure how this kind of oddity fits into the general pattern about ley lines and Flying Saucers. The book seems to fade out on a question mark which, like the smile of the Cheshire cat, hangs in the air after the rest of it has vanished.

Lethbridge could have provided him with one intriguing theory about the nature of apparitions like the one encountered by the young couple. Lethbridge's view is that they are a kind of 'tape-recording'.[2]

We can see that the tape-recording theory would have provided Holiday with a plausible explanation of the corpse-in-the-road. But would it have thrown any light upon his speculations about ley lines and Flying Saucers? The answer is probably yes. Many ley enthusiasts have suggested that the earth-force may be associated with 'supernatural' occurrences. Lethbridge himself was inclined to believe that 'ghosts' (and another type of manifestation which he called 'ghouls'—meaning an unpleasant feeling associated with some spot) were 'recorded' on the electrical field of water, so that a ghost is more likely to be seen in a damp than in a dry place. He also thought that there were similar fields associated with mountains, woodlands and wide-open spaces such as deserts. All this seems to suggest the Chinese 'dragon' force and John Michell's leys. So, what is being suggested is that places in which the earth force is unusually strong—for example, crossing points of ley lines—may 'record' tragic events (or events associated with some strong emotion) far more efficiently than places where the force is weak. And if Holiday is right in believing that UFOs may originate in some 'other dimension' or parallel universe, then these places of high earth-energy would be the places where we would expect to hear of manifestations of Flying Saucers. And, according to Holiday, of lake monsters....

So, in the final pages of *The Dragon and the Disc*, Holiday had taken a bold step into the unknown, but was still a long way from formulating any general theory that might explain the mystery. He was fortunate that he had no reputation to lose. He mentions an American academic who told him that doors had been slammed in his face ever since it was known that he was investigating the Loch Ness Monster. Many respectable journals had praised *The Great Orm of Loch Ness* as a balanced, clear-headed attempt to summarise the evidence. With *The Dragon and the Disc*, he had crossed the line that divides serious monster-hunters from the lunatic fringe. Yet he had no doubt whatever that his conclusions were as sane and balanced as those of the earlier book. What he urgently needed was some general theory that would embrace all the strange phenomena he had encountered. And, as *The Goblin Universe* shows, the last six years of his life were a continual struggle to formulate such a theory. His decision to leave the book unpublished—or at least, to rewrite it—seems to indicate that he felt that his attempt had been a failure.

Holiday was experiencing a problem that is familiar to students of the paranormal. They begin as more or less open-minded sceptics, prepared to give serious consideration to any evidence that presents itself, but determined not to indulge in any self-deceptions. Finally, the sheer weight of evidence convinces them that something odd is going on, and they try to create what Aldous Huxley called a 'minimum working hypothesis', an explanation that covers the basic facts. This may be, for example, telepathy. Lethbridge saw a 'ghost'—a man dressed in riding gear—in the rooms of a university friend, and theorised that someone else may have been thinking about the man, and that his own mind somehow 'picked up' the image—like "...a television picture without the sound." But he was forced to drop this explanation as he encountered other examples of the paranormal. And this tends to be the experience of most serious investigators. Whenever they have formulated a watertight 'general theory', they stumble upon some new fact that simply refuses to fit in. And they have to extend the theory. Then they find still more awkward facts and extend it still further. And in no time at all, their original neat, symmetrical theory looks like an old sack stuffed with rubbish.

This was Ted Holiday's experience, and it explains why *The Goblin Universe* begins with a sentence that sounds like a confession of failure:

"We inhabit a strange cosmos where nothing is absolute, final or conclusive. Truth is an actor who dons one mask after another and then vanishes through a secret door in the stage scenery...."

In fact, he is merely expressing a conviction that strikes every paranormal investigator sooner or later: that the universe probably contains other intelligences besides our own. When the Society for Psychical Research was formed in 1882, a group of distinguished philosophers and scientists hoped to study 'the paranormal' with the same scientific methods they used for studying meteorites or bacteria. They were, in fact, successful to a remarkable degree, establishing the reality of telepathy, clairvoyance, precognition and psychokinesis beyond all possible doubt. But their investigations into the problem of life after death were far less successful because their results were so contradictory. If ghosts and poltergeists really existed, then they seemed determined to confuse the investigators with false information. G. K. Chesterton, who devoted some time to experiments with the Ouija board, agreed that the seances produced unexplainable results, but added: "The only thing I will say with complete confidence about that mystic and invisible power is that it tells lies."

This has also been the experience of many investigators of the UFO phenomenon. The experiences of the American journalist John Keel—which fascinated Holiday—seem to be typical. He became interested in the phenomenon as early as 1945, two years before the pilot Kenneth Arnold started the Flying Saucer craze with his sighting of a number of Unidentified Flying Objects against the background of Mount Rainier, in Washington state. He started off as a sceptical investigator, but in 1954 saw his first UFO at Aswan, in Egypt. In 1966, he became sufficiently interested in UFOs to subscribe to a press cutting agency. The results astounded him; sometimes he received as many as 150 clippings a day. It seemed that there were far more 'sightings' than was generally realised. Many witnesses spoke of being pursued by Flying Saucers as they tried to escape in their cars, and of seeing them later over their homes. Keel's first response was that most of this was probably hysteria or lies; but he decided to interview as many witnesses as possible and was soon convinced that the majority were not liars or publicity seekers (these, he said, were fairly easy to spot), but ordinary, honest people, who were often reluctant to discuss their experiences. Then, in October 1967, as he was driving along the Long Island Expressway, he noticed a sphere of light that was running parallel to his car in the sky. When he arrived at his destination, the 'UFO' was still there, and it had been joined by four others; crowds of people were staring up at them. Keel described the results of his investigation in a book called *Operation Trojan Horse* (1970), and he admits that he has come to accept the 'paraphysical' explanation of UFOs—that they are, in some sense, non-physical objects, who have something in common with the angels and demons of mediaeval tradition, and something in common with such 'paranormal' phenomena as poltergeists and apparitions. Keel also speaks of the mysterious 'men in black' who often plague UFO investigators; in *Operation Trojan Horse* he reports that he interviewed many people who had been contacted by 'men in black' and warned to keep silent about their experiences; sometimes the mystery men were dressed as Air Force officers.

"I quickly discovered, to my amazement, that these 'Air Force officers' all looked alike. They were slight, olive-skinned men with Oriental eyes and high cheekbones. Some witnesses said they looked like Italians; others thought they were Burmese or Indian."

Five years later, in a book called *The Mothman Prophecies* (1975), Keel revealed that he himself had become the object of attention of some of these mysterious entities. He began to investigate sightings of a seven-foot figure with red eyes and folded wings, whom he called Mothman. This had been seen at an old explosives dump in West Virginia. When Keel and three other people went there at night, they had a typically confusing experience. In a deserted building, a girl named Connie—who had previously seen the 'Mothman' figure—suddenly became hysterical, claiming she had seen red eyes looking at her from the darkness. She was taken outside, and Keel rushed back into the building with his electric torch; it was, of course, empty. When he got outside again, the others thought they had seen someone running away into the darkness. They had also heard a loud noise like a heavy piece of metal falling from a height; Keel had heard nothing. Another girl's ear began to bleed. When the others had left, Keel decided to return to the dump for another look. At a certain point on the road, he was suddenly engulfed with fear. A few yards further on, the fear vanished as quickly as it had come. He returned to the same spot; the fear began again. He found that he could walk into it and out of the other side, and that the moment he stepped into it, he experienced a sense of panic. Keel decided that it was due to some 'ultrasonic waves', and when he returned the next day, the 'fear' had gone. Tom Lethbridge had made a similar observation about the entity he called a 'ghoul'; it seemed to be a highly unpleasant feeling—of danger or foreboding—that surrounded places where something 'nasty' had happened. And it was possible to step into it and out of it again as if it had a sharply drawn boundary....

Keel goes on to describe how he was subjected to a peculiar persecution by the 'space men'—mysterious phone calls, warning messages, absurd hoaxes. On one occasion, he chose a motel at random for the night, and found a sheaf of incomprehensible messages waiting for him at the desk. And finally, he began receiving phone calls from a man who called himself Apol, who made a number of curious prophecies. Some were accurate, some were not. Apol mentioned that Robert Kennedy was in great danger, and that the Pope would be knifed to death in the Middle East; shortly before this assassination, there would be a great earthquake. Kennedy was, of course, assassinated. The Vatican announced that the Pope would visit Turkey, and an earthquake there killed a thousand people. But he was not assassinated; what happened was that a madman tried to stab the Pope to death at Manila airport two years later but was overpowered.

Investigators who have studied precognition—for example, Alan Vaughan[3]—have concluded that entities who claim to be spirits of the dead *do* seem to have a certain power of prophecy. But it seems to lack accuracy, as if the future events had been glimpsed in some bewildering kaleidoscope that jumbled up past and future. Psychical investigators are also familiar with the phenomenon of 'earth-bound spirits', who seem to exhibit a malicious sense of humour and—as Chesterton observed—to tell lies. Keel's general conclusion seems to be that Apol—and his fellow 'men in black'—are such entities.

I have devoted a chapter of my book *Mysteries* to examining some of these confusing phenomena. Andrija Puharich's book about Uri Geller is full of them: 'mechanical' voices speak from the air, recording cassettes appear and disappear, car engines stop suddenly and start just as unexpectedly, mysterious spacecraft appear in the middle of nowhere, strange coincidences occur, objects are 'teleported' from one place to another.... It all leaves the reader with a sense of irritated bewilderment. There are moments when he suspects that if these 'extra-terrestrials' are real, then they are determined to cover their trail by producing a series of 'miracles' that are so absurd and meaningless that no normal reader can take them seriously.

In fact, after Puharich and Geller went their separate ways, Puharich continued to be contacted by 'spirits' who claimed to be extra-terrestrials, and who claimed that their immediate aim was to prepare mankind for a mass landing of spacecraft on 'planet earth' My friend Stuart Holroyd became involved in the group of investigators who surrounded Puharich, and told me of some of his own extraordinary 'paranormal experiences' in Tel Aviv—'apports' and similar phenomena. But although the 'extra-terrestrials' gave a highly convincing account of themselves, and of the history of the human race, the great landing on planet earth failed to materialise, and Holroyd's *Prelude to a Landing on Planet Earth* seems to be just another example of the kind of confusing phenomena that surround UFOs and 'earth-bound spirits.'

In *Operation Trojan Horse*, Keel mentions that at the beginning of his career, he was hired by a woman to type a book describing her conversations with an ancient Roman called Lucretius. He materialised in front of her—in his toga—as she was strolling along Riverside Drive one afternoon and talked to her at length about religion and philosophy. He may, of course, have been merely a hallucination. Or he may have belonged to that class of 'communicators' who have been recorded since the early days of spiritualism, and who claim that their aim is to 'bring wisdom to mankind'. In the 1850s, a French savant who was intrigued by the phenomena of spiritualism studied the automatic writings of two sisters who seemed to be excellent mediums and asked 'the spirits' a whole series of questions about the meaning of the universe; the result, *The Spirits' Book*, by Allan Kardec, is still regarded as a classic of its kind. So are the communications recorded in the 1890s by the Rev Stainton Moses and published under the title *Spirit Teachings,* after his death. More recently, the teaching of 'Seth', as recorded by Jane Roberts, have gained an audience of dedicated admirers. In England, a group who call themselves 'The Atlanteans' devote themselves to propagating the teachings of a 'spirit' who calls himself Helio-Arcanophus, who speaks through a man called Tony Neate and who claims to be an inhabitant of ancient Atlantis. In America, a twelve-hundred-page work called *A Course in Miracles* has become something of a best-seller; it was taken down in automatic writing by a professor of psychology named Helen Schucman. None of these 'teachings' can be dismissed as nonsense; yet I personally find it equally difficult to regard them as the inspired outpourings of beings who have achieved a higher level of wisdom than the rest of us. And when Jane Roberts produced a book that claimed to be the 'after death journal' of the philosopher William James, I had no hesitation in dismissing the 'communicator' as another of G. K. Chesterton's liars. The study of such communications leads to the conclusion that they vary from brilliantly perceptive moral insight to feeble-minded gibberish. If we give the 'mediums' the benefit of the doubt and assume that all the communications are genuine—that is, are not simply concocted by frauds—then we are left with the conclusion that some denizens of the spirit world are near-geniuses and others are imbeciles. (The same applies, of course, if the source of the communications is some alter-ego in the unconscious mind.) The conclusion would seem to be that, where communications from the 'other world' are concerned, it is always sensible to look a gift horse in the mouth.

It would seem that Ted Holiday was unfortunate enough to excite the attention of some of these peculiar entities after getting himself involved in the exorcism of Loch Ness; at least, this is his own theory. It came about when he read a letter in a newspaper from the Rev Donald Omand [4], who is an exorcist. His newspaper controversy about the monster led Ted Holiday to write to him. The result was the exorcism of Loch Ness, as described in this book—an exorcism that left them both oddly exhausted. Two days later, Ted went to visit some friends, the Carys, and mentioned that he meant to go and examine the place in the woods where a Swedish journalist had seen a grounded UFO. Mrs Cary and her husband had also seen an orange-coloured ball of light over Loch Ness, and Mrs Cary warned Ted against going to the place where the grounded UFO had been seen. The journalist, Jan-Ove Sundberg, claimed to have been harassed by 'men in black' after he had returned to Sweden, and had suffered a nervous breakdown. Holiday tells how, as Mrs Cary was giving him this advice, there was a rushing sound, like a tornado, outside the window and a series of violent thuds; Ted saw a pyramid of blackish smoke whirling outside. Mrs Cary saw a beam of white light which focused on Ted's forehead. Basil Cary, who was standing with his back to the window pouring a drink, heard nothing and saw nothing. The garden proved to be empty and perfectly normal.

The next morning, as he walked out of the house, Ted saw a 'man in black' who appeared to be waiting for him—the man was dressed in black leather, with goggles and a helmet.

Ted walked up to him and turned his eyes away for about ten seconds; in that time, the man vanished. One year later, near the same spot, Ted had his first heart attack—he describes looking over the side of the stretcher and seeing that they had just passed over the spot where he had seen the man in black. Five years later, Ted died of another heart attack....

All this, of course, proves nothing whatever. The man in black may have been an ordinary motorcyclist who simply walked out of Ted's range of vision. The crashes in the garden may have been an ordinary burst of wind, and Basil Cary may not have heard it because he was slightly deaf. I know that Ted himself was shaken by some of the underwater photographs taken in the 1970s, and began to wonder whether the monster might, after all, turn out to be simply an unknown animal. (This, I suspect, was the reason that he decided to suppress the present book.) Yet when we have looked at all the natural explanations, there is still a great deal that is unexplained—for example, Sundberg's sighting of a UFO and 'men in black'. The thuds that were unheard by Basil Cary remind us of the crash of falling metal heard by everyone but John Keel at the old ammunition dump. It seems to be 'the Pan effect' described in the sixth chapter of this book—the inexplicable terror which can cause climbers to run for their lives—or sailors to jump overboard.

In my book *The Psychic Detectives* I have quoted the philosopher and psychical researcher William James, who at the end of his life confessed that, after twenty-five years of investigation, he still felt that he had made no real advance. He added: "I confess that at times I have been tempted to believe that the Creator has eternally intended this department of nature to remain baffling...", pointing out that although the evidence for ghosts and clairvoyance cannot be explained away, it also seems to remain tantalisingly beyond the bounds of actual proof. This, I have suggested, might be christened 'James's

Law'—the mandate that seems to assert that the evidence for life after death (or any other mystery of the paranormal) shall always be strong enough to reassure the converted, but never conclusive enough to have the slightest influence on unbelievers. This seems to be roughly what Ted Holiday meant when he talked about 'the goblin universe'.

Yet it seems a pity to take this rather defeatist attitude. It is perfectly true that, more than a century after it was founded, the Society for Psychical Research has failed to do what it set out to do: to prove once and for all whether there is life after death. Yet the achievements of the Society have been very real indeed. Before 1882, any sceptic could argue that the evidence for clairvoyance, telepathy, apparitions, doppelgangers, and precognition was virtually non-existent: that it all amounted to a compendium of old wives' tales. Within twenty years, the Society had collected thousands of well-authenticated accounts of all these phenomena. And although sceptics continued to dismiss the whole subject as beneath contempt, serious students of the paranormal knew that they were merely displaying stupidity and ignorance. Professor James Hyslop—a close friend of William James—wrote with understandable exasperation:

"I regard the existence of discarnate spirits as scientifically proved, and I no longer refer to the sceptic as having any right to speak on the subject. Any man who does not accept the existence of discarnate spirits and the proof of it is either ignorant or a moral coward. I give him short shrift, and do not propose to argue with him on the supposition that he knows nothing about the subject."

The real problem, I would suggest, is not lack of evidence, but lack of an overall theory to explain the evidence. This is what Ted Holiday was searching for all his life, and this is what he unfortunately failed to achieve. The present book is full of interesting testimony to his own experience of the paranormal. But he was trying to complete a jigsaw puzzle when half the pieces were missing. The second chapter of this book—on Gilles de Rais and Edward Paisnel—seems to me to display the weakness of his method. There is a great deal of interesting evidence suggesting the reality of reincarnation (and I have discussed this in the relevant chapter of my book *Afterlife*). But it seems to me to serve no purpose to sketch the career of Gilles de Rais, then to outline the crimes of the Jersey rapist, and to suggest that Paisnel may have been a reincarnation of Gilles de Rais because of a number of odd coincidences. It convinces no one—even the 'believers'.

The truth is that Holiday's viewpoint changed completely between the mid-1960s and the mid-1970s, and *The Goblin Universe* is an attempt to sketch the 'new look' universe in which he found himself in the mid-1970s.

I thoroughly sympathise with Ted Holiday, and the predicament he found himself in after writing *The Goblin Universe*. He had started off with a perfectly sensible and scientific curiosity about the Loch Ness monster—and, to a lesser extent, with UFOs. And, little by little, he was forced to admit that his common-sense explanations failed to fit the facts. For a man of his pragmatic temperament, it must have cost a great deal of mental struggle to associate himself with dear old Donald Omand in exorcising Loch Ness. (Nothing would have persuaded me to get involved with the project.) And then, at this point, it began to look as if new investigations of the Loch would show that the monster was, after all, a creature of flesh and blood....

In the event, of course, nothing of the sort has happened, and the Loch Ness Investigation Bureau seems as far away as ever from actually proving the existence of some large, warm blooded creature in the Loch. Yet I cannot help feeling that this is also slightly beside the point. For what we are really talking about here is not the existence or non-existence of some prehistoric survival, but about two radically different views of the world. When he wrote *The Great Orm of Loch Ness*, Ted was inclined to believe that we shall one day be able to explain the universe in terms that would have satisfied Isaac Newton or August Comte. What began to dawn on him as he struggled to understand the strange phenomena he encountered was that this 'scientific' view of the universe may be as naive as the mediaeval belief that the earth is flat and stands in the centre of the universe. He was not really becoming an 'occultist'. He was becoming a wider, less limited sort of scientist—closer, let us say, to Werner Heisenberg or Arthur Young or Fritjoff Capra than to Newton and Comte. Basically, it would not have *mattered* if the Loch Ness monster had been conclusively proved to be a plesiosaurus or giant slug; his view of the universe would have remained as valid as ever.

What Holiday and I are both suggesting is that our whole view of the universe is undergoing a change as radical as the change from mediaeval cosmology to that of quantum physics, and that when this change is complete, we shall see that the new cosmology is not less, but *more* 'scientific' than the old one. No one is trying to revive old wives' tales and mediaeval superstitions; this new cosmology only amounts to a recognition that the *mind* plays a far more active place in the universe than the scholastic philosophers supposed.

This view was expressed, with admirable clarity, as long ago as 1969 by Dr Lawrence LeShan in a little book called *Towards a General Theory of the Paranormal*, and the central point it makes seems to me to be the foundation of the 'new cosmology' whose outline we can sense in *The Goblin Universe*. LeShan points out that every human being has his own 'individual reality' (he shortens it to IR), and that the individual reality of a man who is born blind and deaf is quite different from that of the rest of us. And anthropologists are now beginning to realise that the 'individual reality' of many 'primitives'—for example, the Hopi Indians—is radically different from that which Western man feels to be natural and logical. And he goes on to point out that the individual reality of a mystic seems to be quite different from that of non-mystics —particularly scientists. The mystic seems to feel that time is unreal, that there is a better way of gaining information than through the senses, that there is an underlying unity in all things—so my sense of my 'I-hood' is somehow false—and that evil is merely an appearance. The rest of us are inclined to dismiss such statements as merely 'symbolic', which is another way for saying we think the mystic is stretching the truth. G. E. Moore countered the statement that time is unreal by pulling out his watch, while Dr Johnson 'refuted' Bishop Berkeley's arguments about the unreality of matter by kicking a stone.

But where the paranormal is concerned, there is one very powerful argument against 'common sense' and in favour of the mystic: the evidence for precognition. The annals of the Society for Psychical Research are full of thousands of examples of people who have literally foreseen the future. Precognition simply defies all our attempts at a scientific theory. No presupposition about telepathy, clairvoyance, or the paranormal powers of the right brain can explain how anyone could anticipate something that *has not yet happened*. It is simply impossible. We cannot even begin to imagine how it might be possible to foretell the future with any accuracy, any more than we can imagine a fifth dimension of space, or the concept of nothingness. It seems simply absurd and illogical. *If* genuine precognition exists, it proves that there is something radically wrong with our notion of time, and that in this respect at least, the mystic's reality is closer to the truth than the scientist's. The same point was made by the philosopher Bergson—in fact, it constitutes the central recognition of his philosophy.

Bergson argued that when we grasp something with the intellect, we *cannot help* distorting it, like a strong man trying to pick up some tiny, fragile object. The chief problem with the intellect is that it maps out its object in space and tries to grasp reality in terms of numbers. But you have not explained the beauty of a sunset by talking about the wavelength of its light rays, just as you have not defined the greatness of a symphony by talking about the wavelength of its sounds. A mathematician tells us that a straight line consists of an infinite number of points, and our intellect tells us this is true; but our eyes see a *continuous* line. Our intellect tells us that a minute consists of an infinite number of moments; but we experience time as a continuous flow. This curious limitation of the intellect leads to paradoxes like Zeno's arrow. Consider an arrow in motion. At any given moment it is either where it is or where it isn't. But it can't be where it isn't. And if it's where it is, then it can't be moving.... The old paradox of Apollo and the tortoise also makes use of the intellect's failure to grasp the nature of motion and proves beyond all doubt that Apollo can never overtake the tortoise....

To try to grasp reality with the intellect is like trying to eat soup with a fork, or like trying to pick up a jelly with the claw of a mechanical digger. The intellect simply isn't made for the job — we have to use the intuition.

If we can grasp that what our senses tell us is only limitedly true, we can begin to grasp why the rigidly sceptical view of the paranormal is pathetically inadequate. A few years ago, a group of scientists and stage magicians (including 'the Amazing Randi') formed a society whose chief job was to debunk the paranormal — it called itself CSICOP — Committee for the Scientific Investigation of Claims of the Paranormal; one of its founders was the eminent physicist Professor John Wheeler, who had been cheered at the 1979 meeting of the American Association for the Advancement of Science when he demanded that 'parapsychologists' should be thrown out of 'the workshop of science'. The aim of CSICOP—its members soon became known as Psi-cops—was to reduce the universe to a strictly materialistic model, in which there is no telepathy, no clairvoyance, no precognition, no psychokinesis—and, most emphatically, no life after death. This is, of course, a fairly easy assignment: all you have to do is to firmly refuse to look at any of the overwhelming body of evidence that has been accumulated over the past century, and to insist that anyone who can accept such evidence is childishly gullible. The problem with this attitude is that it also entails a narrow and rigid 'reductionism' about science itself. Life was an accident produced by the action of sunlight on carbon, and every step in its evolution can be explained in terms of Darwin's survival of the fittest. And any suggestion that the universe revealed by quantum physics is not unlike the universe as described by the mystics is rejected with fury. But as science itself shows an increasing tendency to abandon the old mechanical models— speculating, for example, about an eleven-dimensional universe —this attitude becomes increasingly hard to defend, and its advocates look and sound increasingly like members of the Flat Earth Society. It begins to look highly probable that the CSICOP mentality will eventually collapse as a result of its own innate contradictions.

I suspect that Ted Holiday decided not to publish this book because he felt he had failed to achieve his objective—that is, to present an unanswerable case for 'the Goblin Universe'. Most readers will agree that he was being over-critical; his intuitive, 'impressionistic' method of sketching out his case is in many ways more effective than a water-tight but slow-moving argument. Since his death, the emergence of new evidence and new attitudes has continued to strengthen his case, and it now seems probable that, in a decade or so, his views will seem balanced and rather cautious. In the meantime, because Ted Holiday was an intransigent individualist who will always appeal to other individualists, I have no doubt that his delightfully idiosyncratic way of expressing them will give a great deal of pleasure to an audience of discerning readers.

**Notes:**

[1] See Chapter 4. *Ed.*

[2] See also Chapter 4. *Ed.*

[3] See Alan Vaughan's *Patterns of Prophecy*, Turnstone Press, 1974.

[4] See Chapter 6. *Ed.*

# 16

# Introduction: *Lord Halifax's Ghost Book* (D76)

by Charles Lindley, Viscount Halifax
London: Bellew Publishing, 1989.

When Lord Halifax's *Ghost Book* was first published in 1936, two years after the death of its author, it must have struck its readers as a delightful relic of the Victorian era. And this, in fact, is precisely what it was: Charles Lindley Wood, the second Viscount Halifax, had been born in 1839, and was in his ninety-fifth year when he died.

Now, when Charles Wood was nine years old, a momentous event occurred on the other side of the Atlantic in New York State.* In a farmhouse inhabited by a family named Fox, a series of loud rapping noises kept everyone awake at night. A neighbour who was called in to hear the noises concluded that they were being made by some intelligent agency, and asked it to reply to questions with a code of knocks—one for yes, two for no. The 'spirit' identified itself as a pedlar who had been murdered by the previous tenant by having his throat cut—and buried in the basement. Soon, after this, the bangs and raps—typical of what the Germans called a poltergeist, or noisy ghost—turned into a normal 'haunting', with sounds of a death struggle, horrible gurgling noises, and of a body being dragged across the floor. Eventually, the 'spirit' informed its hearers that it was proclaiming the dawning of a new era and ordered them to announce this truth to the world. This is why, on 14 November 1849—when Charles Wood was ten years old—the first 'Spiritualist' meeting took place, and, within months, the new 'religion' had spread across the United States, then across the sea to Europe. And young Wood, who was then at Eton, was so fascinated by it that he and a group of friends engaged in a session of 'table-turning'—which is to say that they sat around a table with their hands in contact, and asked. 'Is anyone there?' According to the author of his obituary, J. G. Lockhart, the results were so 'gratifying' that Wood lay awake with his candle burning for most of the night.

He might have gone on to become one of the most eminent 'psychical researchers' of the age, but fate had other plans for him. He was sent to Oxford, and there became fascinated by the greatest religious controversy of the time: that between the 'High Church' party and the 'Broad Church' party. Past religious controversies usually have a smell of mildew, but this one is, in many ways, still as exciting as ever. It began in 1828, when a young vicar named John Henry Newman began to preach in St Mary's, at Oxford. His conviction that religion was dying out in Victorian England gave his sermons an extraordinary power and passion, and he soon had hosts of enthusiastic followers. Newman should have been born in the Middle Ages, when the Church was the intellectual citadel of civilisation, not the poor, battered, old spokesman of 19th-century Christianity.

By the time Charles Wood came to Oxford, in 1857, Newman was in disgrace, having, in 1845, justified the gloomiest predictions of his enemies by joining the Roman Catholic Church. But 'Newmanism' was as alive as ever. Many of his disciples had become vicars in the slums of industrial cities, where conditions were appalling. The half-starved poor had little use for the dull, conventional worship of the Church of England. The slum priests recognised that the Roman Catholic Church of Spain and Italy had the right idea, with its colourful incense, genuflexions, pageants, and dramatic rituals—making the sign of the cross, sacraments with wafers and wine.... And their flocks responded enthusiastically to the colour and pageantry. The rest of the Church of England was horrified. They suspected the 'Ritualists' of wanting to let the Pope in by the back door. "No popery!" was still a powerful cry in England. There were all kinds of attempts to suppress 'Ritualism'—by Royal Commissions, Acts of Parliament, organised petitions, even legal proceedings. In 1874, a number of Ritualist priests were even sent to prison. (And that, of course, was the turning point; the British, with their love of fair play, began to feel sympathy for this persecuted minority.)

Charles Wood was caught up in this great religious controversy on the side of the Newmanites and Ritualists. He became friendly with Edward Pusey, the man who had inspired Newman. Like so many young Oxford men of the period, he was gripped by a passionate desire to 'serve' in the Franco-Prussian War. It led him to join the Red Cross and serve in France, and in 1886 he worked in the slums of Whitechapel during the cholera epidemic. He could have spent a pleasant and comfortable life as a wealthy English gentleman; he was a close friend of the Prince of Wales and became a Groom of the Bedchamber when he came down from Oxford in 1862. He could have become a distinguished politician, like his maternal grandfather, who was Prime Minister. Instead—to the dismay of his family—he became president of the English Church Union, a 'Newmanite' organisation, at a time when the Ritualists were under violent attack, and he even decided to resign his position as Groom of the Bedchamber in order not to compromise the Prince of Wales. During the remainder of his life, he became identified with the cause that we now call ecumenicalism—the attempt to create a union between the Church of England and Rome—and in 1920 inaugurated a series of dialogues with the archbishop of Malines, Cardinal Mercier, in which responsible Anglicans and Roman Catholics met to discuss their differences.

This helps to explain why a man so passionately interested in ghosts failed to become an active member of the Society for Psychical Research—formed in 1882 on the instigation of a group of Halifax's Oxford contemporaries. But why was he so interested in 'the supernatural'? One clear hint is contained in his entry in the *Dictionary of National Biography*: that three of his four sons died young. Such a tragedy must certainly have deepened his interest in the questions that he states at the beginning of his fictional 'Colonel P's Ghost Story': "Where are the dead—those who have loved us and whom we have loved.... Are they gone from us for ever, or do they return?" But at the end of the same story, where he formulates more speculations on the problem of 'spirits of the dead', he adds:

"The question may not be decided in our present state of existence, nor does the Psychical Society perhaps adopt the most likely way to resolve it. Ghost stories divided into classes, and tabulated under various heads, do not carry conviction."

Now this is certainly an extraordinary statement from someone who spent his life collecting ghost stories. All the Society for Psychical Research tried to do was to answer precisely those questions formulated by Lord Halifax. It set about this task by trying to decide whether 'ghost stories' could be dismissed as pure nonsense and superstition, or whether there was strong factual evidence for them. This task had already been vigorously undertaken in the 1840s by a remarkable lady novelist named Catherine Crowe who, in 1848, had produced an unusual work called *The Night-Side of Nature*, an attempt to review the evidence for 'the supernatural' (or, as we would say, the paranormal) in a scientific manner.**

By the late 1860s, serious thinkers such as Henry Sidgwick and L. H. Myers (both of Oxford) were asking whether 'psychical research' could not be placed on a scientific foundation. Alfred Russel Wallace, one of the founders of the theory of evolution by natural selection, and a brilliant young Irish scientist, William Barrett, also played an important part in creating this new scientific approach. And one of the first major achievements of the Society for Psychical Research was the vast work (over 2,000 pages) called *Phantasms of the Living* by Myers, Gurney and Podmore, which documents hundreds of extraordinary examples of ghosts, as well as of the 'doppelgangers' (or 'doubles') mentioned in the title. So, in fact, the Society for Psychical Research was doing, on a more ambitious scale, exactly what Lord Halifax was doing. One of the main criticisms of Lord Halifax as a collector of ghost stories is that he made so little attempt to sort the wheat from the chaff. A typical example is the story called 'The Shrouded Watcher' included in the second volume of the *Ghost Book*. It was printed in *Blackwood's Magazine*, and purports to be the recollections of an army officer stationed in Malta. He tells of a young gambler called Ralph D—who acquired for himself a reputation as a hell-raiser. According to the author, he returned one night to the barracks, where a regimental band concert had been given, and noticed a tall man in a long, dark, cloak standing under one of the mess windows. The stranger remained visible from the narrator's room. Then, from the open window of the mess, the narrator heard sounds of a quarrel about cards; D— was accused of cheating and was heard to invoke the Devil "to the ruin of his soul and body" if what he said was not true. Whereupon the cloaked figure made a leap through the open window and reappeared a few moments later with D— slung over one shoulder. D—, it seemed, had dropped dead immediately after invoking the Prince of Darkness....

The tale is not made any the less absurd by the additional information, supplied to Lord Halifax by a certain Major White, that the story was originally told by Dr Edward Pusey—whom we have already met in connection with Newman—and that D— was not an army officer in Malta but an under-graduate at Oxford. The 'shrouded watcher', according to Major White, was seen by Dr Pusey himself. Except in grand opera, the Devil does not go around dragging off to hell the souls of sinners who have taken his name in vain.

The same odd kind of gullibility appears in the account of the death of Lord Tyrone, as told by his sister Lady Beresford. It seems that the brother and sister were brought up as Deists— Deism being a religious movement which accepts a Supreme Being but declines to believe that God personally wrote the Old and New Testaments. It would be a pity to spoil an excellent ghost story by summarising it; suffice it to say that when the brother's ghost appeared to his sister, it was to tell her that Deism was false, and that true salvation can only be found through the 'revealed religion' of the Holy Scriptures. No doubt Lord Halifax, as a High Anglican, could accept this salvationist view.

Now there can be no doubt that many readers will feel that this whole subject of ghosts is an absurdity, and that in this sense there is little to choose between this story and any other. I must admit that I have never been able to accept such a simplistic notion. My own view of the matter, based upon twenty years of listening to personal accounts of the paranormal, is much the same as that of the Scottish critic Andrew Lang, who remarked that most people who have seen ghosts are not imaginative hysterics, but "steady, unimaginative, unexcitable people with just one odd experience". Most of the ghost stories I have heard from those who experienced them have been oddly inconsequential and seem to have no 'point'. In the late 1950s, my friend Bill Hopkins took an old gardener's cottage near Battle in Sussex and told me that he and several other people had had a similar experience there: a feeling, when they were in the garden, that someone was looking at them from an upstairs window; many had seen a face looking out. Presumably, it was the ghost of the gardener, but the story has no outcome and no sequel (except that I used it in an early novel called *The World of Violence*[†]). Another friend told me of an old house whose kitchen corridor was haunted by a smell of frying onions. A Mevagissey couple told me that both of them had encountered the ghost of the previous tenant on the upstairs landing, and that neither had been afraid because he was obviously such a nice old man. I was particularly interested in this latter account because at the time, in the mid-1970s, I had just come upon a theory that seemed to me to explain the whole problem very satisfactorily: the so-called tape-recording theory. This was, as far as I know, first formulated by Sir Oliver Lodge around the turn of the century in a book called *Man and the Universe*. Lodge's suggestion was that strong emotions could be "unconsciously recorded in matter" (much as sound can be recorded on a wax cylinder or an iron-oxide tape). This seemed to me an excellent, non-superstitious view of ghosts, one that avoided the necessity of believing in life after death. However, my encounter with the Mevagissey couple introduced an element of doubt into my mind. Both seemed quite certain that the old man had looked *at* them and had reacted to their presence.

It was precisely to try to answer this question that the Society for Psychical Research had been formed in 1882. Their basic method was to try to set up 'laboratory conditions' for spirit mediums, to determine once and for all whether they were cheating, and—when someone claimed to have seen a ghost or had some other paranormal experience—to get signed depositions from everyone concerned, to eliminate exaggeration or downright untruth. (This, we shall see, is a method that Lord Halifax pursued whenever possible—for example, in the case of the Renishaw coffin.) Now, obviously, the fact that two witnesses tell the same story is no proof that it is true. But what soon became clear, as the SPR collected hundreds—and finally thousands—of such accounts, was their extraordinary consistency. Because of this, it became possible to state, with some degree of confidence, whether someone's ghost story was true, or whether it was an invention. We have already seen that, by any standard of common sense, the story about the gambler being dragged off to hell by the Devil was fairly certainly an invention. (It bears all the hallmarks of a horror story by Le Fanu or one of his Victorian contemporaries.) The same, on the whole, applies to the story of Lord Tyrone: it could well be true that Lady Beresford saw her brother at the time of his death— *Phantasms of the Living* contains dozens of such accounts—but the detail about the sinews of the wrist shrivelling as the ghost touched them is undoubtedly nonsense. There are a number of fairly well-authenticated stories of encounters with ghosts in which some kind of physical contact has occurred, and there is no suggestion in any of them that muscles become shrivelled— this episode sounds like a vague echo of stories of 'the Devil's mark', the place on witches that was supposed to be insensitive to pain after being touched by a demonic familiar.

Because Lord Halifax made no attempt to 'tabulate' his ghost stories and 'divide them into classes'—and apparently preferred to ignore the Society for Psychical Research, which had attempted to do so—a number of his tales are simply unbelievable; or downright preposterous. It is difficult, for example, to know why he decided to include the absurd shaggy dog story of the Bordeaux Diligence in his collection, except as a joke. The tale of the Vampire Cat also seems rather dubious. As to the story of the Passenger with the Bag, it bears all the hallmarks of pure invention. If we are to judge by thousands of cases in the SPR records, 'real' ghosts do not get on trains, carrying apparently solid bags of money; they do not leave solid cigar cases behind on the floor; they do not pass on messages to their nieces (to whose house, by an odd coincidence, the narrator happens to be on his way to spend a weekend). It is unnecessary to add that there is no record of the murder of a railway director named Dwerringhouse, or of the trial of another director charged with his robbery and murder. The sceptical reader may feel that such a farrago of nonsense should not, on any account, be taken seriously.

But this would be unfair to Lord Halifax. In fact, many of his stories are well-authenticated, and others bear all the hallmarks of being factual. The 'doppelganger' case of the Revd Spencer Nairne is a good example. It is told by Nairne himself, and it has that odd note of irrelevancy that is so typical of true tales of the paranormal. Nairne was strolling through Aberdeen with a friend when he thought he passed an acquaintance called Miss Wallis, walking on the arm of a gentleman. When he turned to speak to her, she was gone. Miss Wallis also saw Nairne walking in Aberdeen with a friend, and when she turned to speak to him, he was no longer there. But when they later compared notes, it emerged that they had been there on different dates, he on 31 May—as recorded in his diary—while she had been there in July and had *her* diary to prove it.

Nairne apparently sent his account to Frederick Myers, one of the most eminent founders of the Society for Psychical Research. And what Myers said goes straight to the point. He could accept that Miss Wallis had seen Nairne on the spot where he had been a few weeks earlier, but he found it very hard to believe that Nairne could have seen her before she was there. Miss Wallis's experience is consistent with dozens of accounts of 'doppelgangers' in the records of the Society for Psychical Research. In his autobiography, Goethe tells how he was walking home one day after a heavy shower and saw his friend Friedrich walking in front of him, wearing Goethe's own dressing gown. When Goethe arrived home, he found Friedrich standing in front of the fire wearing the dressing gown—he had been on his way to see Goethe when he had been caught in the rain; the housekeeper had lent him Goethe's dressing gown while his own coat dried out. Here it seems clear that Friedrich was thinking of Goethe, and somehow projected a telepathic image which Goethe mistook for reality.

To explain how Miss Wallis thought she saw Nairne, we merely have to assume some close link between them, at least—

as we would now say—of 'being on the same wavelength'. Then the 'tape recording' theory would account for the case quite adequately: Miss Wallis walked over the spot where Nairne had been a few weeks earlier; both were strangers to Aberdeen, and some psychic faculty—the equivalent of a bloodhound's sense of smell—enabled her to 'pick up' his scent, so to speak.

But what about Nairne's vision of Miss Wallis, seen six weeks or so earlier than her visit to Aberdeen? Well, both the Scots and the Norwegians have their own peculiar version of the doppelganger, known as the 'vardoger' or forerunner. Goethe himself relates how, when he was leaving his ladylove Frederika in a mood of deep gloom, he encountered his own double riding in the opposite direction, dressed in a distinctive grey suit with gold embroidery. Eight years later, returning along the same road, Goethe realised to his astonishment that he was now wearing the grey and gold suit, and that he had foreseen his own 'future self'. In a curious modern case, a New York importer named Erikson Gorique went to Norway for the first time in 1955 and was greeted by the hotel clerk as an old acquaintance. A wholesale dealer also recognised Gorique as someone he had met two months earlier, Gorique's 'vardoger' had apparently preceded him.

So the Nairne case, while undoubtedly strange, has a certain air of authenticity. Besides, one of the first things I came to realise when I began to study the 'occult' was that time is not the simple one-way street we naturally assume. Professor Joad, in discussing the curious case of the ladies at Versailles who saw the place as it was in the time of Marie Antoinette, talked about "the undoubted queerness of time". We not only find the notion of accurately foreseeing the future incomprehensible—we find it absurd. Yet hundreds of convincing cases could be cited. Moreover, 'chaos theory' assures us that it is scientifically impossible. Neither the weather nor anything else can ever be predicted more than a few days ahead because every new circumstance that arises causes the future to go off on an increasingly different tack. Laplace once stated that if some super-mind (such as God) could grasp the entire present state of the universe in all its complexity, it would be possible to predict its whole future. Chaos theory says that is not so—that a butterfly flapping its wings in Siberia can change the weather pattern a month hence. But Spencer Nairne's experience, like thousands of others in the records of the SPR, contradicts chaos theory.

As to the ghost stories that form the main substance of the book, there is little to say except that most of them have the same marks of authenticity as so many of the stories collected by the Society for Psychical Research. For example, the story of the haunting of Hinton Ampner is exceptionally well-authenticated. According to Peter Underwood's *Gazetteer of British Ghosts*, the trouble started when, after the death of his wife, Lord Stawell had an affair with her younger sister. Legend accuses her of having borne him a baby, which was murdered. Soon after his death in 1755, the ghost of Lord Stawell was reportedly seen by a groom. Ten years later, the house was let to Mrs Ricketts, who described the haunting in letters to her husband in Jamaica; the letters are quoted in this book.

*Lord Halifax's Ghost Book* is a strangely mixed bag, but since its publication in 1936 it has firmly established itself as a classic, and a favourite even with people who, in the last analysis, insist that they do not believe in ghosts. I regard it as a privilege to introduce it to a new generation of readers.

**Notes:**

* See also Chapter 5. *Ed.*

** See Chapter 11. *Ed.*

† Recently reprinted by Valancourt Books with an Introduction by Nicolas Tredell. *Ed.*

# Preface: *The Intelligent Universe* (D18)

by David Foster
New York: G. P. Putnam's Sons, 1975

In the late autumn of 1970, I received a letter commenting on my autobiography, *Voyage to a Beginning*. Like most writers who deal in ideas; I get a couple of dozen letters from strangers every week—some informative, some polite, some downright abusive. I find that replying to these cuts into my time, so there are occasions when I wish I had the courage, like the philosopher Whitehead, to decide to ignore all correspondence. (Whitehead argued that if he wrote letters, he would do less creative thinking and that this would be a waste of his capacities.) But there was something about this letter that held my attention: a certain air of competence and seriousness, a feeling that the writer knew what he was talking about. Halfway down the page there was a passage in capital letters which I found rather baffling:

"THE UNIVERSE IS A TOTAL CONSTRUCTION OF WAVES AND VIBRATIONS WHOSE INNER CONTENT IS 'MEANING', AND MAN IS A MICRO SYSTEM OF THE SAME VIBRATORY NATURE FLOATING AT SOME DEPTH IN THE UNIVERSAL AND MEANINGFUL WAVE SYSTEM. THE UNIVERSAL WAVE SYSTEM IS QUALITATIVE OR VALUE-STRUCTURED (THIS IS QUANTUM THEORY) ACCORDING TO ITS VIBRATION-RATE SPECTRUM (FASTER FREQUENCIES HAVE MORE INFORMATION CAPACITY)."

This had a religious ring, yet from the rest of the letter, it was clear that the writer was not religious or devoted to occultism. On the contrary, he was a cybernetician who had written—and had published—various technical books. He had been a member of the Gurdjieff-Ouspensky group for thirteen years, which was a fair guarantee that he was not some kind of religious crank. So I devoted half an hour to a careful reading of his letter, and of the "essay" he included with it, the text of a speech he had delivered to an international congress of cyberneticians.

A few weeks before, I had finished writing a 250,000-word book called *The Occult*. The essay and letter made me decide to recall the manuscript, to insert some of the ideas of this remarkable cybernetician. His name was David Foster.

I must first try to explain why I found his ideas so exciting. Although I have written a dozen novels, most of my work is concerned with philosophy—and particularly with existential philosophy. And you could say that the starting point of existentialism is this quotation from Kierkegaard's novel *Repetition*:

"One sticks one's finger into the soil to tell by the smell what land one is in; I stick my finger into existence—it smells of nothing. Where am I? Who am I? How did I come to be here? What is this thing called the world?... How did I come into the world? Why was I not consulted?... And if I am compelled to take part in it, where is the director? I would like to see him."

There is the essence of existentialism: the cry: "Take me to see the director!" And, of course, it does not take most modern philosophers long to reach the conclusion that there is no director. We think in terms of a "director"—or boss—because we are born into a family and get used to parents and figures of authority who create a meaningful world around us. We make the mistake of thinking that the universe must have the same pattern. The naturalist Lorenz pointed out that baby birds and animals make an analogous error; if you place newly born chickens in a cage with a tortoise, they will treat the tortoise as their mother, and cheep pathetically if you take it away. They will even become emotionally attached to a stone. And this, according to certain philosophers, is how we come to imagine that the universe has meaning or purpose; our life-instinct will not allow us to see it for what it really is: a gigantic stone.

Kierkegaard did not take that bleak view; but then, he was a Christian. Later existentialists—Sartre and Heidegger, for example—decided that his Christianity was merely another example of the pathetic fallacy and threw it overboard. So, according to them, human beings are helpless, warm little creatures in a universe that is unaware of their existence; "...it is meaningless that we live and meaningless that we die," says Sartre. All we can do is make the best of one another and of our brief, meaningless lives....

Now I was never able to accept this kind of pessimism, whether preached by the Buddha, Schopenhauer, or Sartre. I could understand their point: that we *want* to see meaning in the universe, like some over-affectionate mother who refuses to accept that her son is a useless bum. But that did not seem to me to *prove* that life is meaningless. Being English I was inclined to approach the problem in a pragmatic manner. I noted that in certain moments of intense happiness—perhaps at Christmas, or on holiday, or in a moment of great relief—we *see* the world as a deeply meaningful place. The next morning the glow has faded, and everything looks as it usually does—a bit *too* solid, too real... and rather boring. And in that state of mind, your moment of insight seems an illusion. But why leave it at that? Most healthy people have these moments of intensity fairly often—say once a month. They are so pleasant that we tend to accept them and enjoy them, without bothering too much. I decided that I would fight this tendency: that every time I experienced this sense of relaxation and power and expansion—the feeling of being connected to some source of power, meaning, and purpose—I would do my best to decide whether it *was* just a 'feeling' a mere warm glow, or whether I was really catching a glimpse of *real* meanings. And, every time, I reached the same conclusion. The experience was too authentic to be wishful thinking. The 'meanings' were really there, not illusions. What was finally so convincing was that these meanings always seemed to be the same; they didn't change. It was as if you went to the top of a church tower and always saw the same view; it couldn't be a mirage. For me, therefore, there was a simple problem: how to *pin down* that meaning, like memorizing a telephone number, so you could recall it the next morning; when the intensity had gone. And this, in turn, meant asking a number of questions that had always concerned philosophers: What are 'meanings'? How do we distinguish between reality and unreality? How can I tell if I am 'kidding myself'?

I went into the question very thoroughly, read all the writers who had dealt with it: pessimists like Schopenhauer, Andreyev, Beckett; optimists like Carlyle, Shaw, Wells, Chesterton; 'in-betweeners' like Nietzsche and Dostoevsky. My first book *The Outsider* (1956) went very thoroughly into this question of whether life must be regarded as meaningless and considered the views of dozens of thinkers and artists from the Buddha to Tolstoy. Toward the end of the book, I considered men whose view tended toward optimism: Blake, Ramakrishna, Shaw. And one of the most prominent in this group was a man who regarded himself as a 'doer' rather than a thinker, George Ivanovich Gurdjieff. Gurdjieff felt that our main trouble is habit—habit that is so deep that it dominates our perceptions and actions, so we cannot throw it off. Habit makes us passive; our problem is to develop the strength to throw it off, and to keep on throwing it off. Gurdjieff had developed various exercises for this purpose. Everyone has noticed how, if they are enjoying a party game—perhaps a relay race or a word game that demands speed and alertness—they feel more awake, more alive. In effect, Gurdjieff's exercises and dances were elaborate party games.

At a slightly later stage, I discovered the work of the psychologist Abraham Maslow, who was primarily interested in *extremely healthy people*, and in what he called 'peak experiences'—which were my own 'intensity experiences', the moments when the world glows with meaning. Maslow observed that healthy people have the most peak experiences, and that this is because they keep the will alive and active. When you are passive, sluggish, depressed, your vital energies sink, and the world actually *looks* meaningless....

All this explains why I was so immediately impressed by David Foster's theories. For he approached this question of meaning as a scientist. Cybernetics is the science of control and communication—basically; how to make a machine behave as if it could think for itself. A weathercock on a steeple is perhaps the simplest example. Because its tail is bigger than its head, it points into the wind. But that is all it *can* do—respond to wind pressure. A player-piano goes through a far more complicated series of motions—it can play 'Pop Goes the Weasel' or Beethoven's Egmont overture—because it is controlled by a sheet of parchment with holes punched in it; these holes are all basically the same device as the large tail and small head of the weathercock. An electronic computer may use cards or tapes punched with holes, but, again, the principle is the same.

What so impressed me about David Foster's theory was the biological, or genetic, part. For he pointed out that all living creatures are created from a code. The 'piano roll' that determined the colour of my hair and the shape of my nose is contained in the genes and, in recent years, has been identified as the DNA molecule. As a cybernetician, David Foster recognized that the DNA molecule is basically a piece of 'coding'. An acorn, for example, could be regarded as a computer card. When you look at a "finished" oak tree, all its material has been taken from the ground and sucked from the air; yet all that carbon, nitrogen, and oxygen has been organized into a definite shape. What organized the shape was the computer code contained in the acorn. What David Foster wanted to know was: Who coded the acorn?

Up to this point, the argument sounds very like 'Paley's watch'. The theologian Paley remarked that when he looked inside his watch, he recognized purposive organization that proved the existence of a maker; but man is a thousand times as complicated as a watch—does not this prove that men must have a Maker? The Darwinians replied: No. It all happened by chance, and by the law of survival of the fittest.

It is certainly arguable—on mathematical grounds—that the complexity of the DNA molecule could not have been produced by purely mechanical laws. Such an argument would not convince a Darwinian, who would reply that man's limited mind cannot conceive the immense complexity of the laws of nature. But David Foster's argument does not rest there. He goes on to point out that one of the basic laws of physics—and cybernetics—is that a highly complex *process* requires even more highly complex *energies* to set it up. You can see, for example, that a watchmaker's tools must always be finer and subtler than the works of the watch; an ordinary engineer's tool kit would be completely useless to him. A conductor's thought processes must always be several steps ahead of those of the orchestra. If an orchestra wanted to play a joke on an inexperienced conductor, it would only have to play faster than he could conduct. And, similarly, the intelligence and energies used in setting up a cybernetic code must always be higher than the code itself.

But, says David Foster, the complexity of the DNA molecule is so great that there are no energies on earth of sufficiently high frequency to 'set it up'. But there *are* plenty of energies in the rest of the universe—cosmic rays are only one example. It is therefore quite possible that the energies that carry the coding come from 'out there' Perhaps there are higher life-forms on the stars beaming out these complex signals; or perhaps the universe itself may not be a dead thing, as scientists assume; perhaps it is alive and intelligent.

If all this sounds suspiciously cranky, rather like the theories of Emanuel Velikovsky or Erich von Däniken, let me put the argument into David Foster's own words, taken from a paper delivered at the Cybernetics Congress in 1972:

"...I put forward a new theory of the universe which suggested that the universe was something like a gigantic electronic computer and that the energetical and material interactions could be regarded as a sort of cosmic data processing.... Since man is a part of the intelligent universe then it would be reasonable to suppose that he incorporates cybernetic design principles; and indeed, a cursory examination of the structure of the human psyche and body indicates a system basically capable of achieving steersmanship.... [This latter word means cybernetic control—the Greek *kybernétés* means a 'steersman'.]"

However, let me state flatly at this point that although I think this idea of David Foster's is interesting and exciting, and quite possibly true, it is not the *foundation* of his thinking. If it was disproved, it would make no real difference to what he has to say. For what really interests him is the complex mechanism of the human mind. Gurdjieff's basic principle is: Study the machine. The machine is the 'mechanical' part of man. In the processes of everyday living, we are like car owners who know how to drive a car, but do not have the first idea of how the engine works. And why should that matter? Because my machine is so bloody *inefficient*. In those moments of intensity and insight, I suddenly realize that most of my life is wasted. The first time

I ever took a real holiday, cycling from Leicester to the Lake District, I kept thinking: "Incredible! England's a fascinating place, and I had to wait until I was eighteen to discover it!" And all the school holidays I had spent in Leicester struck me as an appalling waste. Moments of insight produce the same feeling. Ouspensky once compared man to an enormous mansion, full of picture galleries, libraries, courtyards; yet human consciousness lives in a single basement room and is quite unaware of the rest of the house.

David Foster's achievement is to bring together his training as a cybernetician and his training in self-observation learned from Gurdjieff and Ouspensky. He wants to know how we work and why we work, and how the human machine can be utilized at something like its full potential. And since this is very much my own preoccupation, I find his work—like the present book—full of exciting insight. I may be wrong, but I think the 'foundations' are not necessarily important. In the 1972 lecture he speaks of the Special Theory of Relativity, according to which all physical events must be described in terms of a 'reference system' and an observer at rest in this system. He goes on to argue that "there are no events without experience"—that is, without an observer—and that since the universe is full of events, this suggests that it may have an 'in-built observer' that is intelligent. I am not sure that I grasp the essence of his argument, but I am suspicious of using Einstein in this manner. To begin with, I have never been able to accept the view that events have to be 'relative'; neither have I ever been convinced, to my own satisfaction, that the velocity of light is some kind of limiting velocity. And since this is the very foundation of Special Relativity, I obviously have reservations about the whole theory. But then, David Foster's 'cybernetic analysis' of man does not depend on Einstein or any other theory, only on common sense and minute observation. And this is the essence of his work.

Naturally, I was extremely curious to meet this cybernetic

psychologist. The few things he told me about himself increased the curiosity. He was apparently successful enough in his profession to be able to make a living by working for only a few hours a week, so he could devote the rest of his time to writing and thinking. When Gurdjieff first met Ouspensky, he surprised him by saying that the people who would be best at 'the work' would also be those who were most successful in their everyday lives. It sounds surprising because we are all soaked in the romantic tradition that says that 'great' poets and scientists are usually rather helpless when it comes to the affairs of everyday life. (The really great ones disprove it: Shakespeare became a rich businessman; Goethe was a successful privy counsellor; Shaw was a first-rate vestryman; but we ignore these as exceptions.) Gurdjieff argued that the qualities needed for worldly success—vitality, intelligence, and—above all, 'wide awakeness'—were precisely the qualities needed to shake off the chains of habit, (one of his pupils described 'the work' as "A method for preventing your past from becoming your future.") In that respect, David Foster obviously qualified. He had even invented certain safety precautions in cars ('The Cushion Car')—involving foam padding of different densities—which were in process of being made legal requirements in the United States.

A few months after we had started corresponding, he wrote to say he would be coming to the West Country for a holiday, and we arranged to get together. I suggested meeting in a pub midway between his hotel and our house. Since I had never seen him, I was relying on him to recognize me. On the other hand, many people who have seen early pictures of me—which are still used on some of my books—get entirely the wrong idea: they make me look lean, wolfish, and gloomy, whereas I am, at forty, heavily built, and usually cheerful. So, every time the pub door opened, I looked around and eyed the newcomer enquiringly. Finally, a stranger came in—over six feet tall, with iron-grey hair, a craggy face, and a fawn duffel coat. I moved forward unhesitatingly: "David Foster?" He looked surprised: "No." A few minutes later the real David Foster came in: shortish, round-faced, bespectacled, balding, with a discernible Yorkshire accent. He reminded me slightly of my friend J. B. Priestley—certainly, he might have stepped out of one of Priestley's novels. He was straightforward, un-shy, obviously good-natured; if I had met him in a Bradford pub, I would have taken him for a successful wool merchant—certainly not for the author of the extraordinary typescript on *The Intelligent Universe* that I had been reading.

The general Priestley effect was completed by his wife Min; for Priestley, being an optimist, likes to write about couples who are well suited; and David and wife most obviously were. She struck me as sweet-tempered and very feminine, and intelligent without being in the least self-assertive, a fairly unusual combination. This is also what I had expected. Abraham Maslow pointed out that healthy and vital creatures are usually also good choosers. So I have found it a fairly sound rule to judge a man by the wife he has chosen—obviously one of the most important choices of his life. In this respect, David Foster certainly passed the test.

They came back home with me for supper, and we spent the rest of the evening talking. He didn't bother much about small talk; we got straight down to the important things and stuck with them. It did not take me long to recognize that he is a born phenomenologist—that is, someone who is concerned with the precise *description* of inner-states. And to some extent—I must state at once—we were talking at cross purposes. This was not because we were basically unsympathetic or on different wavelengths. It was simply that he has obviously spent most of his adult life analysing the problems in his own way and developing his own set of concepts and terms for discussing them. There were many points at which his terms and mine overlapped; but there were also many points where I *thought* I understood what he meant, only to realize a few minutes later that I was reading my own ideas into what he had said.

To some extent it was possible to overcome this by speaking in direct, intuitive terms, with a minimum of definition. This comes fairly easily to me because that is the way I think anyway. My basic recognition is extremely simple: I see the paradox of human nature as the fact that we *want* peaceful, happy, uncomplicated lives, yet it is often crisis and danger that gets the best out of us. Peace and quiet *ought* to be good for us; you have only to read an account of some earthquake disaster to realize that. Yet there is something oddly wrong with us so that lack of challenge makes us go to pieces. When a man has been bitten by a poisonous snake, it is best to make him walk up and down; if he falls asleep, he will probably die. And this paradox of human nature seems to indicate that we have the equivalent of snake venom in the system. This is what Gurdjieff meant when he said we are all asleep. It is also what Catholic theologians mean by original sin. The basic difference between my view and the Catholic view is that I am unwilling to believe that it is as serious as that. This is some odd *mechanical* defect in us. Anyone who has ever owned a car with pneumatic windscreen wipers knows what a nuisance they can be if you drive uphill in heavy rain; they slow down and even stop. But it is quite easy to correct this defect by making them work electrically. I have a feeling that the answer, to the human paradox is just as simple.

In fact, in a basic sense, it is. Man is *partly* 'machine' (or robot), partly 'free will'. As I write this, my fingers type automatically, and, to some extent, my brain chooses the words automatically; but the actual thinking about *what* to say must be done by the 'free' part of me. When I am bored, the 'free' part of me tends to relax, and the robot part takes over. When I am happy or excited or faced with crisis, the 'free' part of me comes to the fore. It is as simple as that. Boredom is when the robot is 'winning'; happiness is when 'I' am winning. And so Gurdjieff's system was based on the idea of making his students make enormous *efforts* — perhaps leap out of bed in the middle of the night and instantly do complicated Dervish exercises. In this way, the 'I' part of you is kept in the lead.

But even if you learn this 'trick' — of firmly bullying your own laziness and keeping up a much higher level of effort — you realize that there are still all kinds of fascinating and complicated problems. You are no longer permanently devitalized by useless neuroses; but you realize that there are still further levels of insight to be achieved, deeper levels of freedom. These levels can only be reached by 'understanding the machine'. I think I am right to say that David Foster has himself achieved the basic level of freedom and passed beyond the stage at which most human beings are permanently stuck. He has conquered the psychic country; the next question is to civilize it, to build 'roads and railways' and perhaps eventually 'airports'.

He has brought to this task his training as an engineer and as a scientist. And this seems to me to be the most valuable kind of approach. Many people have as much insight as David Foster (although not *that* many), but they tend to be mostly artistic or religious types — Subuh and the Maharishi come to mind. They gather disciples and teach 'enlightenment'; but no matter how hard they try to be 'objective' they manage to give the impression that everything depends upon joining the group and drinking at the fountainhead. On the other hand, David Foster has the same kind of approach as Shaw or Wells — the feeling that although this knowledge may require a fairly high degree of comprehension, it does not require any special teaching conditions; if you are willing to make the effort, you can learn it in an armchair at home. Gurdjieff falls midway between the two groups; although his basic method is as objective and 'scientific' as David Foster's, he felt that most people are too weak to 'go it alone'. If you make a New Year resolution not to smoke, and you keep it to yourself, the chances are fairly high that you will break it. If you tell everybody you have decided to give up smoking, you stand a better chance of keeping it. But if you join a community of people who have *all* decided to give it up, you will almost certainly succeed. This is the Gurdjieff principle, and it is obviously sound. On the other hand, people like myself and David Foster have the kind of mentality that wants to attack the problem frontally, with the analytical intellect. Being fairly cheerful characters, we are not terribly worried that this amounts to *hubris*. It wouldn't really matter if it did. We enjoy doing it and—at the very worst—it is a harmless pursuit.

I suspect that David Foster's mind is more scientifically oriented than my own, and this emerges in his terminology. But there are no basic differences. Two paragraphs from his most recent letter to me will illustrate this:

"Man needs two things under the bracket of cybernetic intelligence: Your Faculty X which I call 'cybernetic virtue': this is the ability to clear a psychic space inside oneself for autonomy and autonomous initiative. It is a state, the state of self-control. It very much involves watching the inner panorama (what I have been calling 'insight') and separating from it.

"Once one has the taste for it one can do it for long periods. 'Intelligence', which is much concerned with 'knowing what is going on now', is also the ability to plan future life-games with some degree of reality. Perhaps this is where you and I diverge a trifle since for me it is the cybernetic purposeful aspect of man which is more important than the peak experience."

Here I can understand instantly and precisely what he means in the first paragraph: 'Psychic space'. We normally have a certain feeling of being *suffocated*, a perpetual feeling of being in a hurry. Then there are moments when the tension vanishes, and I can suddenly 'breathe'. And his 'watching the inner panorama' is a perfect description of phenomenology.

In the second paragraph, he moves into his own terminology, and in order to understand what he means by 'life games' I have to see that he is contrasting them with peak experiences. The peak experience is the 'moment of vision' in which you can suddenly see your way ahead. (After all, our chief problem is that we live with our noses pressed so tightly against the present moment that we are hardly aware of anything but immediate necessities; and when those disappear, we don't know *what* to do next. Instead of making use of the moment of freedom, we fall into boredom.) David Foster is here contrasting the 'moments of vision' with purposeful *action* and asserting that his own preference is for purposeful action. The gap between us here is not as wide as he supposes, but it is worth mentioning because it typifies the difference between our individual approaches. I want to keep returning to the over-all vision; ideally, I would like to keep it all the time; my approach is very intuitive, very 'simplistic'. David Foster is more concerned with getting on with the task of analysis, getting his bridge built; so, he is not afraid to multiply new concepts, to draw analogies from science, and so on.

I am not saying I disagree with this method. Although it may be more complex than my own intuitive approach, it can make for important insights. Perhaps I should offer an example. Looking through Bernard Lonergan's important book *Insight* the other day, I came across this excellent definition of Gödel's proof:

"Gödel's theorem is to the effect that any set of mathematical definitions and postulates gives rise to further questions that cannot be answered on the basis of the definitions and postulates."

It immediately struck me that this is also true for my own basic feeling about the world. At any given moment of our lives, we have a definite *feeling* about the 'meaning of existence'. A man returning from a funeral may intellectualize it and say that it is all a cheat that ends in the grave; a young mother holding her first baby may intellectualize it and say that life is more thrilling and exciting than we normally give it credit for. But, mostly, we do not 'intellectualize' our response to it like this. Nevertheless, there is always a response, a kind of vague opinion about life. When I am very excited or have been struck by a sudden deep insight, I have a feeling of expanding horizons; the 'picture frame' of my opinion melts. I have a sense of facing the sheer *unknown-ness* of the world. If I work hard and try not to forget this vision, I can incorporate it into my basic 'opinion' about life, and the result is a picture with a much larger frame. The 'frame' seems a necessary part of my way of seeing the world; yet when it has dissolved once or twice, I realize that it is an absurdity. Everything that is in the picture implies the existence of new vistas beyond it; the frame is really a liar. Yet I cannot grasp the world without it; such is the nature of mind.

This seems to me to be a fairly important insight, and it comes as consequence of stumbling across the definition of Gödel's theorem. But I have a feeling that if I did this too much, my work would become altogether too complicated; better skip the intellectual parallels and stick to the basic insight. I am inclined to half-suspect that David Foster would not only introduce Gödel's proof into the argument, but that he might also use it as a proof that the 'dissolving picture-frame' view of the universe is supported by mathematical theory....And he *could* well be right. But while my own plodding mind and limited intuitions decline to allow me to *see* that far, I prefer to forget the whole thing and return to my simple image of a man suffering from snakebite.

But these are minor reservations and qualifications. About

the basic quality of his work, I have no doubt at all. In his tough-minded, analytical way, he keeps grabbing the problems by the throat and wrestling with them. While the Love Generation and the LSD crowd preach the importance of feeling instead of thinking, he continues unrepentantly to think and to achieve by calculation the moods of insight that they may achieve by accident. He has solved one of the major problems about safer motor cars—he once told me that he did it by filling electric light bulbs with sand and dropping them from different heights on to pads of foam rubber—and now he is determined to apply the same common-sense, pragmatic approach to the problem of 'original sin'. He is not primarily a writer—which is to say that he is not too concerned about impressing his readers with brilliant paradoxes or tricks of style—and the result is that he conveys an exciting impression that anybody could learn to think creatively.

Oddly enough, Bernard Shaw recognized that people like David Foster would appear. In *Man and Superman,* he makes Tanner speak jokingly about the New Man. Everybody talks about the New Woman whenever some particularly old-fashioned female comes along, says Tanner, but nobody has noticed the arrival of the New Man—typified by his chauffeur, Enry Straker—the cool, efficient engineer who corrects Tanner when he ascribes a Beaumarchais quotation to Voltaire, and who certainly knows more about the devious ways of women than his employer. Enry is a joke, but it has a substratum of seriousness. Shaw's first successful novel (artistically speaking), written at the age of twenty-three, treats the character with more depth; the hero of *The Irrational Knot,* is an engineer and inventor called Edward Conolly, who dominates the novel with his peculiar blend of common sense and intellectual insight. A few years later, Shaw introduced the New Man into his first successful comedy, *Arms and the Man,* in which the romantic hero is a Swiss-hotel-keeper-turned-professional-soldier. More than half a century later he was still obsessed by the New Man and introduces him into his last three plays: *Farfetched Fables*, *Why She Would Not*, and *Buoyant Billions*, the last of which ends with a great speech in praise of mathematics. Shaw recognized the inadequacy of the romantic artist as an evolutionary type— the everlasting inefficiency and self-pity. He saw that it would be harder to endow poets with practical sense than to endow practical men with vision and evolutionary drive; and that this may well be the next development in the human type. I do not know how many more David Fosters there are around—he has something in common with Ouspensky and J. G. Bennett, both Gurdjieff students—but I am certain there can never be too many of them.

# About the Authors

**Colin Wilson** was born in the East Midlands city of Leicester in 1931. After the phenomenal success of his first book *The Outsider* in 1956, he moved to Cornwall where he pursued a successful career as a writer, producing over 150 titles in fifty-five years. Essentially an existential philosopher, he has also written on crime, psychology, sex, the occult, literature, music, unexplained phenomena, history, pre-history and over 20 novels in various genres. He died in December 2013.

**Colin Stanley** was born in Topsham, Devon, UK in 1952 and educated at Exmouth School. Beginning in 1970, he worked for Devon Library Services, studying for two years in London, before moving to Nottingham where he worked for the University of Nottingham until July 2005. The Managing Editor of Paupers' Press, he is also the author and editor of several books and booklets about Colin Wilson and his work. His collection of Wilson's work now forms *The Colin Wilson Collection* at the University of Nottingham, an archive opened in the summer of 2011 and which now includes many of the author's manuscripts. He is the convener of the bi-annual Colin Wilson Conference.

# Index

Book titles are in italics with those by Colin Wilson marked (CW)

A major publishing event by *O-Books* marked Colin
Wilson's 80th birthday in June 2011—the tribute *Around the
Outsider: Essays Presented to Colin Wilson on the Occasion
of his 80th Birthday*

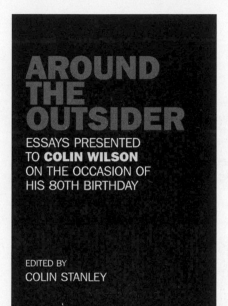

This landmark book of 345
pages, which collects 20
essays by academics, authors,
and other key commentators
internationally, is edited by
freelance writer Colin Stanley,
Wilson's bibliographer and the
managing editor of Paupers'
Press, featuring extended essays
on Wilson's work by scholars
worldwide. Colin Stanley also
provides the preface and two
essays.

Contributors from the
UK, USA, Australia and New
Zealand have written on their
favourite Wilson book, or one which has special significance for them. The
outcome is a diverse and indispensable assessment of Wilson's writings
on philosophy, psychology, literature, criminology, the occult, and
autobiography over more than 50 years, with critical appraisals of four of
his most thought-provoking novels. The line-up includes three professors,
Thomas Bertonneau (literature), Stephen Clark (philosophy) and Stanley
Krippner (psychology), the author and critic Nicholas Tredell, the author
and former editor of the literary magazine *Abraxas*, Paul Newman, the
author Gary Lachman, and Steve Taylor, a lecturer and researcher in
transpersonal psychology. Other contributing authors include Simon
Brighton, Antoni Diller, Chris Nelson, David Power, Philip Coulthard of
*colinwilsononline.com*, journalist Geoff Ward, who established and runs the
*Colin Wilson World* website, Murray Ewing, of the David Lindsay website

at *violetapple.org.uk*, and George Poulos. The novelist Laura Del Rivo, a contemporary of Wilson, contributes an appendix, as does writer and poet Vaughan Robertson, and author Terry Welbourn with a personal appreciation of Wilson and T C Lethbridge.

ISBN: 978-1-84694-668-4

The 'Occult Trilogy' is the collective label applied to Colin Wilson's three major works on the occult: *The Occult* (1971); *Mysteries: An Investigation into the Occult, the Paranormal and the Supernatural* (1978) and *Beyond the Occult* (1988). They amounted to a monumental 1600 pages and have spawned many other lesser works.

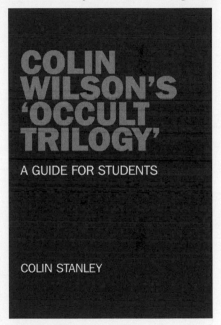

Colin Stanley, Wilson's bibliographer and editor of *Around the Outsider: essays presented to Colin Wilson on the occasion of his 80th birthday* (O-Books, 2011) and the 'Colin Wilson Studies' series (Paupers' Press, ISSN: 0959-180-X), provides a perceptive analysis of each book, appending full bibliographical details to facilitate further study.

Axis Mundi Books
ISBN: 978-1846947063

"Colin Wilson's 'occult trilogy' offers not only an encyclopaedic account of the mysterious 'hidden' powers of nature and the human mind, as well as a history of our pursuit of them, it also provides a clear guide to how mankind can actualize its inner resources and fulfil its evolutionary destiny. Colin Stanley's thorough and fascinating overview gives the reader a firm grounding in this enormously important subject and lays a solid foundation for its future development." **Gary Lachman**, author of: *The Secret History of Consciousness, Jung the Mystic, Turn Off Your Mind.*

"Insightful and engaging, this is an essential guide for any serious student of Colin Wilson's books." **Steve Taylor**, author of *The Fall, Back to Sanity*

## The Ultimate Colin Wilson

Containing extracts from Colin Wilson's key writings on existentialism, consciousness studies, psychology, criminology, and the occult, this is an invaluable introduction to one of the late twentieth-century's most incisive and challenging thinkers. It is the only book to collect extracts from Colin Wilson's most important work in one volume, including *The Outsider* (1956), *A Criminal History of Mankind* (1984), *Introduction to the New Existentialism* (1966), *The Occult* (1971), *New Pathways in Psychology* (1972) and *Mysteries* (1978), as well as three of his novels and many other texts.

This is a fully updated and revised edition of the classic Colin Wilson collection first published in 1985, which contained Colin Wilson's own selection from what he believed to be his key works. It now includes six essential post-1985 essays and chapters chosen by his bibliographer Colin Stanley and other Colin Wilson experts including Gary Lachman, Nicolas Tredell, Geoff Ward and Vaughan Rapatahana.

**Watkins Publishing**
**ISBN: 978-1-78678-253-3**

AXIS MUNDI
BOOKS

EXPLORING THE WORLD OF HIDDEN KNOWLEDGE

Axis Mundi Books provide the most revealing and coherent explorations and investigations of the world of hidden or forbidden knowledge. Take a fascinating journey into the realm of Esoteric Mysteries, High Magic (non-pagan), Mysticism, Mystical Worlds, Goddess, Angels, Aliens, Archetypes, Cosmology, Alchemy, Gnosticism, Theosophy, Kabbalah, Secret Societies and Religions, Symbolism, Quantum Theory, Conspiracy Theories, Apocalyptic Mythology, Unexplained Phenomena, Holy Grail and Alternative Views of Mainstream Religion.
If you have enjoyed this book, why not tell other readers by posting a review on your preferred book site? Recent bestsellers from Axis Mundi Books are:

**On Dragonfly Wings**
A Skeptic's Journey to Mediumship
Daniela I. Norris
Daniela Norris, former diplomat and atheist, discovers communication with the other side following the sudden death of her younger brother.
Paperback: 978-1-78279-512-4 ebook: 978-1-78279-511-7

## Inner Light

The Self-Realization via the Western Esoteric Tradition

P.T. Mistlberger

A comprehensive course in spiritual development using the
powerful teachings of the Western esoteric tradition.

Paperback: 978-1-84694-610-3 ebook: 978-1-78279-625-1

## The Seeker's Guide to Harry Potter

Dr Geo Trevarthen

An in-depth analysis of the mythological symbols and themes
encountered in the Harry Potter series, revealing layers of meaning
beneath the surface of J K Rowling's stories.

Paperback: 978-1-84694-093-4 ebook: 978-1-84694-649-3

## The 7 Mysteries

Your Journey from Matter to Spirit

Grahame Martin

By simply reading this book you embark on a journey of
transformation from the world of matter into spirit.

Paperback: 978-1-84694-364-5

## Angel Healing & Alchemy

How To Begin Melchisadec, Sacred Seven & the Violet Ray

Angela McGerr

Angelic Healing for physical and spiritual harmony.

Paperback: 978-1-78279-742-5 ebook: 978-1-78279-337-3

## Colin Wilson's 'Occult Trilogy'

A Guide for Students

Colin Stanley

An essential guide to Colin Wilson's major writings on the occult.

Paperback: 978-1-84694-706-3 ebook: 978-1-84694-679-0

## The Heart of the Hereafter
Love Stories from the End of Life
Marcia Brennan
This book can change not only how we view the end of life, but
how we view life itself and the many types of love we experience.
Paperback: 978-1-78279-528-5 ebook: 978-1-78279-527-8

## Kabbalah Made Easy
Maggy Whitehouse
A down to earth, no-red-strings-attached look at the mystical
tradition made famous by the Kabbalah Center.
Paperback: 978-1-84694-544-1 ebook: 978-1-84694-890-9

## The Whole Elephant Revealed
Insights Into the Existence and Operation of Universal Laws and
the Golden Ratio
Marja de Vries
An exploration of the universal laws which make up the dynamic
harmony and balance of the universe.
Paperback: 978-1-78099-042-2 ebook: 978-1-78099-043-9

Readers of ebooks can buy or view any of these bestsellers by
clicking on the live link in the title. Most titles are published in
paperback and as an ebook. Paperbacks are available in traditional
bookshops. Both print and ebook formats are available online.
Find more titles and sign up to our readers' newsletter at
http://www.johnhuntpublishing.com/mind-body-spirit
Follow us on Facebook at https://www.facebook.com/OBooks and
Twitter at https://twitter.com/obooks